Julia Ann Morgan

FOUR YEARS AMONG THE REBELS

A Nashville Woman's Life in
Georgia During the War

by
Julia Ann Morgan
(Mrs. Irby Morgan)

THE CONFEDERATE
REPRINT COMPANY
☆   ☆   ☆   ☆
WWW.CONFEDERATEREPRINT.COM

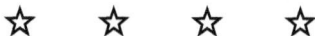

Four Years Among the Rebels
by Julia Ann Morgan

Originally Published in 1892
by Publishing House, Methodist Episcopal Church, South
Nashville, Tennessee

Reprint Edition © 2016
The Confederate Reprint Company
Post Office Box 2027
Toccoa, Georgia 30577
www.confederatereprint.com

Cover and Interior by
Magnolia Graphic Design
www.magnoliagraphicdesign.com

ISBN-13: 978-1945848025
ISBN-10: 1945848022

Dedicated to the Confederate Soldiers

INTRODUCTION
☆ ☆ ☆ ☆

This book gives an inside view of things during the war by a truthful, patriotic, great-hearted woman, whose keen observation and kindly soul are reflected in its pages. It is refreshing, after the deluge of dry official reports of campaigns and battles and the unhappy contentions of so many surviving heroes as to where to locate the glory of victory and the shame of defeat, to hear a woman's voice telling the story of that awful time in her own way, which is very straightforward, circumstantial, and realistic. I mean realistic, not in the nude and vulgar realism of a class of modern novels equally inane and indecent, but realistic in the sense that events are narrated with simple truthfulness. There is no partisan coloring or melodramatic flourish. Mrs. Morgan tells what she saw and heard during those "Four Years with the Rebels" in a colloquial style that suits the theme and charms the reader.

Mrs. Morgan is a Southern woman, and the throb of her womanly heart is in every line. The splendid courage of the soldiers of the Confederacy finds part of its explanation in the intense devotion, unfailing fortitude, and sublime self-sacrifice of the women of the South. The sons and husbands of such women could not be cowards. Even in a case in which cowardice might be in the blood or the nerves, the inspiration of woman's sympathy and the traditions of a people where courage is hereditary, and among whom true chivalry yet lingers in this materialistic and sordid age, the constitutionally timid were swept into the current and carried forward on the crest of the fiery waves of war.

It is worthy of notice that Mrs. Morgan, writing more than a quarter of a century after the war, expresses no doubt of the righteousness of the Southern cause. Whatever may be said of the people of the South, and whatever may be the ultimate verdict of the world, it is uttering nonsense to say that their hearts were not in the struggle. Men do not die and women do not suffer, as the men and women of the South died and suffered, for a cause that is not dear to them. Had not the hearts of the men and women of the South been in the cause, the Confederacy would have collapsed with its first serious reverse. The leaders of the South did not drag the Southern people into the war any more than did the leaders of the North drag the Northern people into it. They had been drifting into its vortex for two generations, and what had been long dreaded and foretold came in 1861.

Reconstruction has been effected, and reconciliation has been so greatly advanced that hopeful patriots of all sections indulge the expectation that the time is not far off when the last note of sectional discord will be hushed, and the last sectional politician will be buried deep with his face downward. But it may be said here, as it has been said before, that if it is insisted that, as a condition of perfect reconciliation, the Southern people shall acknowledge that the boys in gray fought and died for a cause they believed to be wrong, the trumpet of the last judgment will sound before they will make the shameful concession. They were defeated, but they made a good fight for what they believed to be a just cause. They died for their convictions, and no Southern man or woman will seek to fix upon their memories the blot of insincerity. Neither will any true man or woman of the North seek thus to smirch the memory of our dead heroes. The women of the two sections who still mourn for their dead who sleep where they fell may clasp hands in a sacrament of sorrow and forgive on both sides, but they cannot forget.

Within the bounds of Mrs. Morgan's personal acquaintance in Nashville and elsewhere she is well esteemed as a lady of the highest social respectability and Christian virtues. Beyond that circle is the general public, to whom I commend these pages with these "Introductory Words," with the belief that they will greatly enjoy their perusal, and with the hope that, having yielded to the urgent request of her family and friends in giving this book to the press, the author may be rewarded by a large measure of success.

O.P. Fitzgerald.

March 4, 1892.

Irby Morgan

CHAPTER ONE

☆ ☆ ☆ ☆

The people of Nashville for weeks before the fall of Fort Sumter were greatly excited, as the whole country was watching and waiting coming events. Fort Sumter fell; and no one can describe the excitement but one who witnessed it, and every one commenced planning and trying to do something to aid the South.

Drums were beating, fifes playing, the boys coming in troops to enlist for the war, and anxious fathers and mothers could be met at every point. All were earnest and anxious, as few had anticipated the result of the wrangling the country had had for years; and now war was upon us, and we totally unprepared for it.

All the old guns and muskets to be found were brought into requisition, and many consulted as to how to use them, how they could be remodeled, etc., and we of the South were in a dilemma what to do; but we went on the presumption, "where there's a will there's a way," to get us out of difficulty, and the result proved it.

Mr. V. K. Stevenson and others formed a company to gather war materials, and my husband, Mr. Irby Morgan, was selected by him to go to New Orleans, Louisville, and other points to get sulphur and other material for making caps.

Col. Samuel D. Morgan took great interest in the cap factory, and it was a success, for in a short time they were making thousands. Mr. Morgan brought home two of the first perfect caps, and requested me to keep them as souvenirs of the war. The caps that were used at Manassas and Bull Run were made in our cap factory of the material bought by my husband. After this factory had proved a success, Mr. Morgan and others were sent to hunt wool to make clothes for our soldiers, and he went to Texas and other points and bought four hundred and fifty thousand pounds and had it shipped to Nashville, and from here he took it to factories in Mississippi, Alabama, Georgia, and East Tennessee to be made into Confederate gray. He went to the factories and got the cloth, and the last he procured Gen. Rody had to send an escort to guard the wagons, and he delivered to the department in Atlanta five hundred thousand yards of Confederate gray which he had had made at a cost of seventy-five cents a yard, when it was selling in the market at five dollars a yard. After he returned from Texas, then our work began.

Col. Terry's gallant command from Texas came through the marshes of Louisiana, in water and mud almost waist deep, and most of them took severe colds, and by the time they got to Nashville a number were sick. To add to their troubles, the measles broke out among them. Hospitals were hurriedly fitted up, and they were soon crowded. The citizens were greatly distressed, and the ladies went in troops to see them, to take delicacies, and to do all to alleviate their sufferings. Miss Jane Thomas, Mrs. Felicia Porter, and many others were untiring in their attentions; but the hospitals were so crowded and uncomfortable that a number decided to take them to their homes and nurse them. A great many were young, petted darlings at home, and of course they were wretched. I took Capt. Rice, a grand old man who lived on Trinity River on a large farm; also Frank Roan, Capt. Hunter, and Frank Kibbe, all four from Texas, and Levi Jones, of East Tennessee. All were very ill with measles and terrible coughs, and we sent for our family physician and did all we could for them, sitting up and nursing for two months. I hired a nurse and got the boys from the store to help sit up with them. Capt. Hunter was delirious for two weeks, and Capt. Rice as ill as could be to live, and we watched and waited as tenderly as possible.

After two months Capt. Hunter got strong enough to join his command, so did Frank Roan and Kibber; that left me with Levi Jones and Capt. Rice. Dr. Atchison told me he thought Capt. Rice would die. I was much distressed, for I had become greatly attached to the old man. I went to him and said: "Captain, you are very sick; I fear you will not get well."

He said, with a great deal of earnestness and quiet dignity: "Madam, I am an old man. I have plenty at home, a large farm, negroes, no wife nor children, and the boys were all leaving, and I loved them and could not stand to see them go without me, and I thought a country that had done so much for me I ought to fight for it."

I said: "My dear old friend, you must try to think of a better land, to which you are fast hastening. Look to God for help. We have done all we can for you; now beg God to help you to be ready to meet him."

He said: "I have always been charitable, have ever been kind to my negroes, and old Master will deal kindly with me. I have no fears." And just as the glorious sun rose the old man's spirit took its flight, I hope to a better world. We buried him at Mt. Olivet.

All were gone now but Levi. He seemed delighted with his surroundings; would come into my room and would sit for hours with the children and myself and tell me about his mother, sisters, and brothers, and wish he was at home with them. He said he wished he was at home so he could go to the singing school. He was tired of the war. He reverted to the singing school again and again, and said they made the prettiest music he ever heard; indeed they were powerful singers.

One day I said I thought the fresh air would do him good: "I will have the carriage ready, and I want you to take a ride." He was delighted, and observed that he thought it would do him "a power of good." As he crossed the bridge he saw his first steamboat; and he was charmed, and told me when he got home that he thought "it was such a good idea, houses floatin' on water, and a feller could fish all the way down."

He got to looking well and ate heartily, and I said: "Levi, I expect soon they will call on you to join your command."

He said: "Yes; I am looking any day to be sent for, but I am powerful weak." He screwed up his courage enough to appoint a time to join his regiment, but when the fatal day arrived he came to my room with a handkerchief bound around his jaws. I asked him what was the matter. He said his tooth was killing him it was aching so bad. I got him camphor, laudanum, and warm cloths to apply, and he sat with his head bent down in his hands and rocked and moaned and, as I thought, oblivious to all surroundings; but all of a sudden he looked up with his keen, black eyes, and said: "When I go home, I am going to send you a barrel of apples and sweet taters." I thanked him, and said he was very kind; and then he would rock and moan again, seeming in great agony. After being silent for some time, he raised his head again and said: "Miss Morgan, California must be a great country. Sweet taters grows thar an trees, and weighs sixty pounds." I told him I thought it wonderful. He was just nineteen, and could I have done so, I would have sent him home to his mother to be happy. After his toothache was cured he could find no other excuse, so finally, with great reluctance, he joined his command.

Col. Erasmus Burt

CHAPTER TWO

☆ ☆ ☆ ☆

The next startling event was the battle of Ball's Bluff, in which Col. Erasmus Burt, brother-in-law of Mr. Morgan, lost his life. He was Auditor of the State of Mississippi, and raised a splendid regiment around Jackson, sons of the best and most influential families, and went to Virginia to the seat of action. They had a terrific fight there, and Col. Burt killed Col. Baker, of Oregon, and a whole regiment of Federals fired on him, and as Col. Burt fell, mortally wounded, his regiment yelled and charged like demons, killed and drove into the Potomac two thousand seven hundred men, and it was called at the time by the Federal papers: "The Ball's Bluff Disaster." Col. Burt was promoted for his bravery, but it came too late, as he died the next day. This was early in the war, and a company was detailed to escort his remains to Jackson. He was beloved by all, for he was a brave soldier and a Christian gentleman. He left a widow and eight children with no protector, so Mr. Morgan moved them to Alabama near relatives.

One day it was announced that Gen. Beauregard and Father Ryan would give a talk on the war, at Masonic Hall, so we went to hear them. This was soon after the battles of Bull Run and Manassas, and they had a great deal that was encouraging to say. After the lecture was over we went up to the platform and were introduced to them, and expressed pleasure at hearing them give so encouraging accounts of our prospects. Gen. Beauregard spoke of the battles of Manassas and Bull Run, and said the Federals were so demoralized that if we had been prepared to pursue them we could have gone to Washington and dictated terms of peace. He asked my husband if he was related to Gen. John T. Morgan, and he told him he was his brother. He said we ought to be proud of him, for at a critical time in the battle he, by his strategy, helped to turn the tide in our favor. We told him that Nashville had made the caps that fought those battles. I never will forget Father Ryan's noble countenance, so full of love and gentleness. He had long hair, a handsome face, and every inch a man and poet, and his love for our Southland beamed forth in every look and trembled in ever word he uttered.

They had been fighting at Fort Donelson for days, and we would hear very distressing accounts from them: our boys in water knee-deep, and such terrific fighting it was fearful to contemplate, and such overwhelming numbers to contend with. But almost every day we would hear of deeds of valor and bravery, and we felt that our noble boys could not be whipped. They were outnumbered and had to succumb, and only those know, who went through these exciting times, what the news of the fall of Fort Donelson meant.

The next report was that the army was falling back and would make a stand at Nashville. Some said they would fight in Edgefield; others, that they would fall back and fight on the other side of the river. By the next morning the streets were filled with soldiers, wagons, army stores, and artillery wagons being prepared to send South, and the excitement was at fever heat, and pandemonium seemed to reign.

The next news was from an old friend, Mrs. Stubbs, who said Gen. Albert Sidney Johnston was at her home; had come there to rest, and everything was being done for his comfort. I prepared a waiter of delicacies, and was soon on my way to her house. When I arrived, she insisted on my seeing him, but I said I wouldn't think of intruding. She took the waiter to him, and in a little while came back with a message from the general that he would like to see me. She took my arm, and almost before I knew it I was in Gen. Johnston's presence. He expressed great regret at having to fall back. I told him I hoped he would not think it presumption, but I was anxious to know if he intended making a stand at Nashville.

"My husband intends to take us South if the army does fall back; but if it is not proper to answer, don't hesitate to decline. I am anxious to know, for we will have to make some few prepared before leaving home."

He said: "You had better get ready and start in the morning."

I looked at that noble face and massive head, and saw sorrow and care depicted there, and I have never forgotten him. That careworn face is fresh in my memory. I have met Mrs. Stubbs many times since the war, and she loved to dwell on the time Gen. Johnston was at her house, and she, as many others would have done, considered it a great honor to entertain so brave a man.

I went home, and soon after saw Drs. McTyeire and Summers, knowing they were as anxious as we to get away with their families. But by night the rumor was all over town that the army would make a stand, and every one who could shoulder a musket must help to defend Nashville to the last ditch. My husband thought it best for us to go, and he would stay and fight if necessary. So we started to Fayetteville. Before leaving, I called up my two faithful servants, husband and wife, Henry and Martha Brown by name, told them to take the keys, use wood, coal, and contents of the larder, and take good care of the house and everything in it; and faithfully they performed their part. They buried my China, packed at night my carpets to my mother in Nashville, carried my furniture, piece at a time, to the houses of different friends, and stayed as long as they were allowed. The Federals wanted to make a hospital of the house, when our friends, Mr. Dick White and family, moved in and kept it for us till the close of the war. Martha and Henry went to Washington with President Johnson's family, Martha as maid in the "White House," and Henry as a trusted servant; but he died a few months after going there. I mention all this to show the fidelity of the old servants. They had been with us many years, and "Mammy Martha" was dearly beloved by us all. I packed my trunk, took my nurse Ella, and children, and my little son, ten years old, to drive the barouche, and we started to old friends in Fayetteville, leaving Mr. Morgan there to await coming developments. We traveled with sad hearts, thinking of the dear ones left behind who could not follow us.

Events soon showed that instead of making a stand the army was retreating, and the roads were filled with every kind of vehicle of which the imagination could conceive. Artillery wagons, ambulances, furniture wagons, carts, and every kind of conveyance to which a horse could be hitched. They were driving, lashing, yelling, and galloping, and my little children and myself in the midst of them. We got to Murfreesboro after dark, but found that the army had beaten us there and all the hotels were filled. There we were in the crowded street, not knowing where to go or what to do, when I heard my old hackman's voice, Frank Eakin, for he had waited on me in that capacity for many years whenever a hack was needed. Never did a voice sound so sweet! for I was much fatigued, and more worried in mind than body.

He ran up and said: "Is that you, Miss Julia?"

And I said: "Yes; what is left of me."

He said: "I will take you out to Miss Julia Eakin's [Miss Julia Spence, now], and Miss Myra Eakin is there – just come all the way from New York – got there this evening."

So I gladly followed Uncle Frank until we got to Mrs. David Spence's house, and there received a hearty welcome, and we all sat up till late that night, bemoaning the fortunes of war. Early in the morning old Frank had everything in readiness, trunks securely strapped, harness adjusted, etc., and many directions to my son how to drive to prevent an accident. Then, after Mrs. Spence had prepared us a sumptuous lunch, we bade them good-bye, thanking God for having such kind friends raised up to us in our hour of need.

Gen. John C. Breckinridge

CHAPTER THREE

☆ ☆ ☆ ☆

We rode on and on, and I thought our journey would never end. The children would say they heard cannonading, and I would imagine a thousand things were happening, and Mr. Morgan among them, and I felt wretchedly. Just as we rode into Shelbyville the children exclaimed: "There comes papa, on a horse, riding as fast as he can!" I strained my eyes to see, but the dust was so bad that objects directly in front could hardly be distinguished; but sure enough, their keen eyes were not mistaken, for on he came at a rapid gait to catch up with us, and we were all so delighted we forgot how tired we were; and the children's tongues let loose, and such a Babel of voices you never heard, all trying to talk at once, telling our hairbreadth escapes from being run over by so many wagons. We spent the night in Shelbyville, and next day started to Fayetteville to stay with an old friend, Dr. Robert McKinney. Mr. Morgan went on to Atlanta to attend to government business.

When we arrived at Fayetteville, we found a large portion of Johnston's army there, and they continued to come for several days. We met at the doctor's house Gen. John C. Breckinridge, an old friend of the family; Gen.

Forrest; Dr. Kelley (or rather Col. David Kelley), then on Gen. Forrest's staff; and Gen. Bowen and wife, of Gen. Price's army of Missouri. We heard the fight at Fort Donelson discussed from every point, and I came to the conclusion that our soldiers had done enough to stop and not fire another gun. I heard Gen. Forrest tell of the execution of our sharpshooters, and after the battle he said he counted sixty killed in one place, and called on Col. Kelley to know if that was the number. He said their execution was wonderful and fearful to contemplate, the number killed was so great. Gen. Bowen was a splendid specimen of manhood, and his wife was charming. They spent a week at the doctor's, and we had a pleasant time going to see the soldiers drill. Soon the army left for Corinth and Shiloh. I learned that Gen. Bowen was killed at Shiloh, and his wife returned to Missouri.

Before Mr. Morgan left he gave me a box of gold containing $12,000, and told me to take good care of it: we might need it. I told Mrs. McKinney, and we discussed the danger of keeping it in the house, for we felt very anxious about it, as there were servants going in and out all the time. We thought and planned as to the safest disposition that could be made of it. There was a large rosebush directly under the window of her bedroom; so we decided to dig up the rose, divide it, and send a piece of it to a neighbor who was anxious to have some of it, and while the servant went to deliver the rose to our friend we slipped the box in the hole and planted back what was left of the rose, gave it a good pounding and profuse watering, and it scarcely wilted, it was so well managed.

We remained in Fayetteville six weeks, then Mr. Morgan came and took us to Lookout Mountain to Mr.

Aldehoff's Seminary, where we boarded and sent the children to school. Several Nashville girls were here at the seminary. We had a delightful time roaming over the mountains, for the scenery was magnificent; and every afternoon I would take my children and a troop of boys and girls – for both sexes attended the school – and we would walk for miles, feasting our eyes on the beautiful mountain azaleas, holly, and laurel, and many lovely wild flowers which were rare to us, and we would all go back with our hands and aprons full of the sweet blooms. The air was so cool and bracing it seemed we would never tire of these excursions. I was so charmed with the beautiful flowers and shrubs, and so confident we would whip the Yankees and get home by fall or spring at the least, and acting on the presumption, I got some of the mountain women to go with me to select plants to take back to Nashville. I walked, looked, and admired, and tied a piece of white string on one, red and black on others, so I would know them when I got ready to take them up. I planned that I would take up enough native soil to insure success when I removed them, and I was so delighted with the idea of procuring so many novelties I would walk for miles hunting them. But alas! the time never came for them to be transplanted, for after that too much of stern reality occurred to fill the heart and mind, and made me forget the beautiful wild flowers.

In our strolls we would often come in contact with the residents, and would have long chats with them. They seemed well satisfied with their surroundings. Most of them had been reared there, knew but little of the outside world, and were contented and happy. I asked them how they lived, as most of the men were in the army; and they told me they dug calamus, ginseng, and angelica, and gathered huckleberries, blackberries, and dewberries, raised chickens and hogs, and they got on finely. They were kind-hearted, polite, and credulous to a degree that astonished me, and seemed ready to believe all the marvelous tales that could be conceived of. I felt so sorry for them, seeing how ignorant they were; and then I thought they were happier than we were, with no aspirations in life, and thankful for what they had.

One day the children came in and told me that Gen. John H. Morgan's command had just come and were encamped just down the hill; and in a day or two Gens. Morgan and Basil Duke, hearing we were there, came up to see us. Mr. Aldehoff and wife treated them so kindly that they were delighted with their visit. Mrs. Aldehoff was a descendant of Gov. Sevier, and a splendid woman, and her husband a most enthusiastic Southerner.

The boys soon heard we were related to Gen. Morgan, and they came in numbers to see us; and as I had learned most of the patriotic war songs, I would play, and the children and soldier boys would gather around and would make the welkin ring with "Dixie," "Bonny Blue Flag," "Maryland," "She Comes, She Comes." She did not come, but, to judge from the singing, we were very happy in the anticipation. Among the boys was one named Hughes Hopkins, a son of a Presbyterian minister, and the brightest, jolliest fellow I ever met. He formed quite an attachment for the children, and would come up nearly every day to see us. He was highly educated, could quote poetry by the hour, and he was so entertaining we all loved to hear him. One day he was telling us some of his trials on the Potomac, and he said that they were very hungry and had their skillets frying bacon, and were waiting for it to get done when the Federals opened fire on them, and a head of a soldier was blown in their skillet and spoiled all their sop. I told him it was horrible in him to speak so lightly of death. He laughed and said that it was the evil of war, and a fellow gets hardened and used to anything.

The time came for them to move, and he came to say good-bye. He had a splendid form, straight as an arrow, had a pleasant though homely face, and on one cheek was a long scar. He extended his hand, and said: "Good-bye, madam. You have been kind to me, and I thank you, and if I never meet you again, for I may be killed [I felt like crying, his voice was so pathetic], have me decently buried, and please, ma'am, furnish money to have masses said for my soul. I think I will make a pretty corpse." I asked what his good father would say to hear him talk so, and he gave a hearty laugh, raised his hat, and bounded down the hill like a deer. That was the last I ever saw of him. I do not know whether the poor fellow was killed or not.

I was kept very busy with my children, for my faithful nurse I brought with me was taken sick. She was the only daughter of Peggy Lapsley, of Nashville. Her mother came to me the morning I left home, and asked me to take her South, as I could do a better part by her than she could. She relieved me of a great deal of care with my children, day and night. Ella was a bright mulatto, very handsome and intelligent, and I felt in my exile she was more than a servant to me. She almost felt like one of my family, for they were devoted to her, she was so tender and gentle to the little ones. She grew worse day by day, and the physician from Chattanooga pronounced her very ill, and he feared I would have to lose her. She became so nervous that the noise of the children worried her, and I thought it best to have her moved to the house of a poor white family who lived near the seminary, and for a sum of money the mother and daughter promised to devote all their time to her, wait on her faithfully, and sit up with her. I prepared all her meals, had them sent to her, and went every day and stayed with her as much as possible, and would go after supper to see if she had every attention. The school children and mountain woman, seeing our distress, became greatly interested in her, and often after school the children would gather flowers and take them to her. And she was always so grateful.

She lived six weeks, and as she was growing weaker she said: "Miss Julia, I want to ask a favor of you. I know I am going to die, and I feel perfectly resigned, but I hate to leave you and the children."

I asked what favor it was she wished, for I would do anything for her. She said: "Please take all my little trinkets to my mother – breastpin, locket, and some of my hair – and tell her to meet me in heaven."

I promised to do all she asked, and wanted to know if that was all. She said: "No, there is one thing more. Miss Julia, I hate to ask you, but I want you to shroud me. I don't want strangers to do it."

I told her I would do anything for her, as she had been faithful and true to me and mine, and that I would stay by her till the end. She died two days later, and I got a nice coffin and shroud and laid her out tenderly, and as she was lowered in the grave I felt that one of my best friends had left me. We had her buried on the mountain, and the school children came in a procession and covered her grave with flowers. We had a fence built around her grave, and as long as we stayed there her grave was bright with fresh flowers. When I got back to Nashville, I sent for her mother to deliver Ella's treasures to her, but learned that she too had passed to her eternal home, dying near the same time her child did. I go through all this detail to show the devotion of Southerners to their slaves.

The children were anxious to see the sun rise on the mountain, for we had heard what a magnificent sight it was, so we got up quite a party and started early, and we were repaid, for a more glorious sight was never beheld. We were so high above the surrounding country that we appeared, in the dreamy, misty morning, as if we were in fairyland, with the floating, feathery clouds around us. After the sun threw his light in all directions the fleecy clouds began to dispel and the grand old Tennessee appeared like a silver band winding its course placidly along, and cars looked like tiny carriages. As I looked on this grand river I felt like shouting and praising God and saying, "Thou, O Lord, art worthy to receive glory and honor," for such magnificence in scenery I never beheld. We had been on the mountain six months, and had spent the time very pleasantly. We had made many friends among the boys and girls, who were from the best families of East Tennessee and different sections of the country. But the time came for us to leave, as the Federals were thundering their artillery all around Chattanooga, and the reverberations on the mountains were terrific.

Gen. John T. Morgan

CHAPTER FOUR

☆ ☆ ☆ ☆

Mr. Morgan came up to Chattanooga and carried us down to Marietta, Ga., and procured board at the Kennesaw Hotel, and sent to Alabama for his old father and sister and family, consisting of Mrs. Col. Burt and six children. Her two oldest sons had gone into the army. He got a farm close to town, bought three negro boys for her, and had his old father to manage the place. We brought her two daughters in town to go to school with our girls, and they all started to Mr. Benedict, an Episcopal minister, who had a fine school in Marietta. My husband had finished his government business and had joined the army, going with his brother's command, Gen. John T. Morgan's, the Fifty-first Alabama Regiment, as a private. Gen. Clemens and Hon. George W. Jones, two old friends, came to me and told me that it was a shame for Mr. Morgan to go, as he was over forty-five; he could be so much more useful at other points, as good business men were badly needed, and he could do more for the cause by staying in Atlanta than by enlisting as a private.

They and other friends wrote to Richmond to his brother-in-law, Judge William P. Chilton, member of Congress, and Meredith P. Gentry, to state the case; and the next mail brought back a commission as quartermaster of a division, with headquarters at Atlanta. I was delighted, and sent it to him; but it was returned posthaste to Richmond, he declining to accept it.

I was at a crowded hotel, but I got Mr. White, the proprietor, to give me a private table in the dining room for my family and a few friends, among them Mary Gentry, daughter of Meredith P. Gentry, Mr. Fred Shepherd, of Nashville, and Mr. Sandy Shepherd, from Memphis. The latter gentleman was there looking after the interest of his bank. We sent to Charleston and bought a sack of Java, and I got my nurse, Nancy, to make us good coffee on my stove in my room. We fared better than most of them at the hotel tables, for they had parched wheat and rye for coffee; and old friends coming and going soon learned where to get a cup of pure coffee, and Nancy was often kept busy to supply the demand. Judge Caruthers, Judge Marchbanks, Gov. Neil S. Brown, my old teacher, Dr. C. D. Elliot, and many others got their cup as long as it lasted. Dr. Elliot would say: "Julia, my child, I am going up to the front to look after the boys, and must have my coffee to take with me; my supply is out." His knapsack was always filled for him, and he would go off with a glad heart to try and comfort the soldier boys. He was as much devoted to them as he was to his old Nashville Academy pupils, and that was saying a great deal, for he had been a faithful teacher and friend to hundreds of girls scattered all over the South.

Nancy was my courier, always on the alert to get startling news. After the battle of Murfreesboro she came up early one morning and told me the house was filled with wounded soldiers. Their destiny was Atlanta, as they had hospitals there and none at Marietta at that time.

The poor fellows had heard that a great many Nashville refugees were there, and as the train stopped they slipped off in the dark and came to the hotel and sent word to us that they wanted to see the Nashville ladies; but just at the time most of them had left. I got up though, and as soon as I dressed I went down to see them. I went from room to room, and found twenty-seven poor fellows – some terribly wounded – shot in the legs and arms, and one had his eye put out. Different parts of the brave boys' bodies felt the effects of the Yankee bullets. I went in one room, and found Dr. Lowe, from Shelby County, shot through the eye, the ball coming out of the back of his neck, and it was strange that it did not kill him. His hair was very long, all bloody, and dried to his face, and all caked with blood around his eye, or the socket, as the eye was gone. I felt sick at heart, but went to work with my nurse to assist me. I had warm water brought, and with a soft cloth bathed the bloody hair until I could remove it from the wounded part, got a pair of scissors, and soon made the poor fellow more comfortable by cutting off his long, matted hair, and a more grateful man I never saw. He was in a fearful condition, but as I looked at the poor, sightless eye and pleased face I felt repaid for my efforts; and he told me he felt more comfortable and so thankful to me.

I did not take time to hunt help, but went from room to room. The wounded men were all dirty, hungry, and bloody. My heart would give a big bound as I looked eagerly into each face, thinking maybe some of our Nashville boys were among them. I found Capt. Jackson, from the Hermitage, Capt. Lynn and Mr. Herran, from near Memphis, and others, whose names, after the lapse of so many years, I have forgotten, but all in the same condition: dirty, bloody, and hungry. As fare was high at the hotel, and most of the poor fellows were without money, I sent Nancy out, bought light bread, butter, and eggs, and had strong coffee made in my room, and we went to work cooking, and in a little while had enough prepared for them to eat to satiety. The next thing to be done was to get them some clothes. I started and hunted up all the Nashville ladies at the other hotel, and those boarding in town, and also called on the ladies of Marietta to help us. I had a hundred yards of pressed flannel my husband had bought to use in case of an emergency, as goods were getting very scarce; but when such scenes of distress were brought to me, my first impulse was to help relieve, so I got the ladies together and we cut out and made up as long as the cloth held out, and what I lacked others furnished. Hurrying and sewing for several days, we got all supplied with flannel shirts, drawers, and undershirts, and as "cleanliness is next to godliness," they felt nearer heaven in clean beds, and new underclothes, and good women around them ministering to their wants, than they had in some time before.

In the meantime we sent for Drs. Steward and Setz, and they did all they could for their comfort. Mr. White, the proprietor, came to me and said: "I am a poor man and am not able to feed them, but will let them stay until places can be provided for them." I told him I would see to their being fed, and I did; and had them well fed, too. I put on my bonnet and started out to hunt homes in private families for them, and I had good success. Mrs. Gen. Hansel took four; Mrs. Col. Atkinson, four; Mrs. Brumby, three; Mrs. Dennead, three; and so on until all had comfortable homes provided, and I felt happy to know that they would be so well cared for. Most of the ladies sent their carriages for them, and they went with thankful hearts. As they were the first wounded soldiers who had stopped in Marietta, they all fared sumptuously, and Dr. Setz and dear old Dr. Steward visited them regularly and did all in their power to alleviate their sufferings.

Some of the boys were extremely ill from their wounds, as erysipelas set in. I got a home for two country boys who were badly wounded, with an old lady and gentleman who had no children. Two days after, the old lady sent for me to come to see her on important business. I hurried down, called for her, and she said: "You must move those boys from my house, I can't stand them." I asked what on the earth was the matter. She told me her place and all she had was about to walk off with, as the soldiers called them, "graybacks." The neat housekeep was in despair. Allusion to these pests is not very delicate, but they were common in the army, where so many were crowded together they could not help getting them on their clothing. It made no difference how neat and cleanly they were, they were all in the same category, liable to the "pests."

I said: "Please don't move them; one has high fever now and is delirious, and the other is too sick to be disturbed." I got some one to help her clean her house; then sent for a negro barber and told him I would pay him well if he would help me. He asked me what I wanted done, and told him to get a large kettle, heat water, then get a big tub, soap, and towel. He got every thing in readiness and attempted to take one of the soldier's clothes off, and I was waiting to hear the result. The negro came out puffing and blowing, and said: "I can't do anything with him. He fit me and scratched, and tried to bite me." I told him that was a small matter, not to give up, but to go and hire a strong man to help him, for I told him it must be done. He went off for assistance, and in a little while was back with help.

After waiting quite a time, and hearing a big fuss in the room, he came out and said: "Missus, I done soap him and scrub him good, and now he is done dress up nice." I thanked him and told him to go through the same process with the other one. He did so, and had no trouble with him. He came and told me he had finished them both, and I then directed him to cut their hair. This was accomplished, and he sent for me to come in and see how well he had done his work. Strange to say, the delirium was relieved, fever cooled, and they began to improve from that bath. The next thing was to look after their clothing. They each had a suit of Confederate gray, and as clothes were so scarce and hard to get, I could not think of throwing them away. I had them all taken out in the yard and told the barber to go right off and get an old darky to come and wash them. He soon brought an old woman, and, for a stipulated price, she undertook the job.

She looked at the clothes, and said: "Missus, dem's powerful 'ceitful t'ings, dey hides in ebery seam and crack. You has to bile dem all day and all night, and den dey ain't dead."

I told her to "bile 'em all day and all night," just so she got them clean.

"But, missus, dat ain't all; you has to get the hottest flatiron, and iron in all de seams."

I told her I would leave it with her, just so she got them all right, and she worked over them faithfully until they were clean and nice, and hung up for future use.

I went down the next day, and the boys looked like new men, and the old lady was bright and cheerful, and I felt happy at my success. Some of the women of the present day may think it would have been more suitable for men to attend to these things. But where were our men? Most of them were tramping through mud and dirt, rain and cold fighting battles, many lying on the cold ground wounded, and others passed to "that bourn whence no traveler returns." No, when duty led the Southern women, we did not stop to consider if the thing necessary to be done was elegant or delicate, but what ought we do to alleviate suffering, and cool a parching brow, or make a bed softer to the maimed and shattered limbs of our dear ones. Many of them had loving kindred thinking and praying for darling husbands, brothers, and sons.

I thought I had my country charges all settled and happy, but in a few days I was sent for to come as quickly as I could: they wanted to see me. I went down and was received at the door by the old lady. She was very kind, and told me her boys were doing finely, but were somewhat nervous. I walked in and asked if they wished to see me about anything important. They said "Yes," in a low, confidential way, and continued, "I believe the old lady wants to kill us, as she has a loom in the next room, right against the partition at the head of our bed, and she has been weaving for two days, and late last night, and says she has a good deal more to do before she finishes her cloth." I told them I would make it all right; I knew the old lady was good and kind, and I knew too she didn't mean to annoy them. They said: "Yes, she is good to us; gives us plenty that is nice to eat, and talks kindly to us, but that rattle, rattle, rattle [said in a wail] will kill us; we can't stand it." I had a talk with the old lady, and she promised to postpone the weaving, and seemed sorry that she had annoyed them. They stayed with her until they were well enough to join their regiments.

Two days before they left the servant came in and announced two soldiers in the parlor; said they wanted to see me, and I immediately went in. They looked neat, fresh, and cheerful in their suits of gray that the old regress had "biled all day and all night," and to my astonishment, each one had a fiddle under his arm. They said they were going away and thought they would play some for the children and myself; said they were considered "powerful good players" at home. I thanked them for their thoughtfulness, called the children in, then they tuned and tuned, and finally started off on some jigs, and they played all the country breakdowns you ever heard. The more and louder they played, the more numerous became their audience. The children and servants in the hotel came in numbers, until they had a crowd of attentive listeners. As the excitement increased, the louder they played, until they seemed in perfect ecstacy. After they had played all they knew, we all thanked them, bade them good-bye, and it was the last I ever saw or heard of them. On shaking their hands in farewell I felt touched, for the poor fellows had paid what they conceived to be the greatest compliment in life: given me the benefit of what they imagined fine music.

CHAPTER FIVE

☆ ☆ ☆ ☆

Capt. Jackson's wound proved more serious than we thought it would at first. Col. and Mrs. Atkinson and Miss Annie were as kind and attentive as possible, and tried in every way to alleviate his sufferings. Erysipelas set in, and he had raging fevers and was delirious. I went to see him as often as possible, and I feared he would die; but by faithful nursing he began to show signs of recovery, and after some time he was well enough to ride, and Miss Annie would bring him in her carriage to see me, and soon rumor had it that when the captain left he would leave his heart in Marietta.

Mrs. Gen. Hansel had Dr. Lowe and Mr. Herron from Shelby County, Tenn. I mention these three particularly, for they all had erysipelas, raging fevers, and this in connection with their bad wounds gave us much anxiety for their recovery; but the beautiful surroundings of Mrs. Hansel's home, and kind treatment, soon had them on the road to health.

Capt. Lynn, of Tennessee, was badly wounded. He came hobbling in one morning on crutches, and told me his leg was in a terrible condition, and he feared amputation would be necessary. He said he hated to ask me, but he would be so thankful if I would take off the bandage and see what I thought of it. The doctors then were scarce and in great demand all the time. He was wounded just below the knee on the underside of the leg. I got my servant to get me some hot water, Castile soap, and some old linen rags, removed the bandage, and found the place in a frightful condition. His leg was swollen large enough for two, and the cloths had dried and hardened on it until I wondered how he endured it at all. I washed it carefully, saturating the soft linen with some soothing solution the doctor had given him. After the bandage was readjusted he felt much relieved, and I told him to come to me every day and I would dress it for him. He was very grateful, and after the close of the war I got a letter of thanks from him saying I saved his leg. I think that a mistake, but I certainly made him feel more comfortable.

By the most tender care of the ladies of Marietta, and the best medical skill, they all got well and rejoined their regiments. Marietta, up to that time, had known but little of the horrors of war; so the first wounded soldiers they nursed gave them a little insight in it. Soon after this hospitals were established there. Then the work commenced in earnest. We had at this time quite a colony of Nashvillians: Dr. A. L. P. Green, wife and daughter, Mr. Matt McClung and wife, Miss Patty Anderson, Mr. Ike Lytton and family, Mr. Jess Thomas and family, Mr. Tom Marshall and wife, Mrs. Avent, Miss Bettie Childress and her sister, Miss Ann Patterson, Miss Frank Anderson, Gen. Clemmons, Hon. George W. Jones, Mr. Sandy Shepherd, Mr. Fred Shepherd, and many others too numerous to mention, and all great workers. Some one or other of them were always finding objects of distress, and their necessities were always supplied.

Col. John. Overton was there and was as bighearted then as he is now, running up to the army and then back again, speaking words of comfort to the boys at the front and the poor wounded ones in the rear. But enough. I could fill a volume with acts of heroism and devotion to our Confederacy. To sum it all up, we had our hearts and hands full. At this time most of the Nashville ladies were at the two hotels. At the Kennesaw House, where we boarded, the saintly Mrs. A.L.P. Green would appoint one day in each week for fasting and prayer for our beloved cause, and we would try to say "thy will be done," but am afraid we had a mental reservation, "but let us whip the Yankees."

Now the sick and wounded came in numbers, and we were all kept busy trying to minister to their necessities and to the alleviation of their pains. In a short time the town became so crowded many of the Nashville people moved to other points. That left us almost alone at the hotel. Mr. and Mrs. White, the proprietors, were very kind to us, and helped in many ways in caring for the sick and wounded soldiers. The house was full of strangers, coming and going all the time. A family stopped there for awhile that interested me very much. It consisted of Gov. Baylor, of Arizona; Col. Baylor, his brother, our former Minister to Austria; and the Governor's and colonel's brother and sister, Eugene and Fanny Courtney Baylor. Gov. and Col. Baylor were delightful company, and Fanny and Eugene splendid musicians, and every night Mary Gentry and myself got them to play for us. Fanny sang the Scotch songs with much pathos, and some of Eugene's compositions were wonderful. He was only twenty years old, but was wonderfully gifted in music. My girls got him to teach them many pieces of his own composition. I did not think then that these friends we were making would in after years make a name for themselves, for they were so modest and unassuming; but Eugene has lived to be a great composer of music, and Fanny an authoress of considerable note.

On two occasions trains of soldiers came down the road, and we learned that on account of some accidents they had nothing to eat in twenty-four hours. We were all greatly excited, and I went around from one boarder to another and got their consent to give up their breakfast and let the soldiers have it. I told Mr. White, the landlord, our decision, and he agreed to it. I dispatched my nurse to make coffee, and in a little while big and little, white and black were carrying dishes out to the train to feed the soldiers. We took everything in the eating line we could lay our hands on, and as fast as one pot of coffee was emptied I would send for another. It was a long train, and it took a good deal to satisfy the famished occupants. Soon the news got out in town, and a rumor to the effect that there was a trainful of starving soldiers was circulated, and here they came, women and children running, with their faces red from excitement – some with provisions, others directing servants with large waiters, baskets, bundles, and any way it could be brought in a hurry. The soldiers ate like they were starved; and when the whistle blew, such scrambling and grabbing as there was to take what was left with them.

All were bountifully fed and were happy, and with many thanks and loud cheers they were gone; but still tired and almost breathless women continued to come with their donations, and were much disappointed when they found the train had moved off. This was a memorable day in Marietta, but we felt well repaid in going without our breakfast to see the enjoyment depicted in the faces of our soldier boys. In a short time gamblers and rough characters began to come in such numbers that it made it disagreeable for us, but Mr. Morgan was in the army and I thought I would try to stand it, as I was anxious to keep as near the front as possible. Almost every day there were disturbances among these characters, and it made me very watchful. One night I sent my little son to see if supper was ready. The dining room was next to the office, and as he was a favorite in the house, some one called him in the office to speak to him; and this time it happened to be the marshal from Atlanta, and he took him in his lap and was talking to him when a gambler, who supposed he had come up to arrest him, fired on the marshal, killing him, the ball going just above my son's head, and as the marshal fell Bob rolled over on the floor. You can imagine my feeling when some one came up and told me. I was almost frantic, and ran downstairs, but met one of my friends leading Bob to my room. He was as white as a sheet and frightened almost to death. Mr. Fred Shepherd begged me to let him take the children and myself and go to the other hotel, but I told him I would go in my room, lock the door, and not let any one in. I thanked God for preserving my child's life, for it was a narrow escape. I got my nurse and children in my room and locked the door and awaited results with fear and trembling, for we heard that a mob was after the gambler and intended to hang him. And such an uproar in the streets and hotel was fearful. I waited an hour listening to every sound, almost afraid to breathe.

In a short time I heard screams and the sound came nearer and nearer, and some one commenced shaking my door as if they would break it down. I said:

"Who is there?"

Mrs. White, the proprietor's wife, said: "It is I. For God's sake come down, Mrs. Morgan. They have cut Mr. White all to pieces, and I can't get any one to come and help me." The children were attached to Mr. White, who was kind to them and would often assist them in their lessons, as he was a fine mathematician. So I asked them if they would be afraid for me to leave them, and they all said no – to go and help Mr. White and they would stay with Nancy, the nurse, who promised me faithfully not to open the door at all. So I started, but in the meantime Mrs. White had gone back to her husband, and with a prayer for help and protection I ran down the hall and one pair of steps, then another hall until I got to her door, and I said, "Open quickly;" for I was so badly frightened I could hardly stand on my feet. We were soon in the room and the door again locked. The doctor had been sent for, but could not be found, and I told Mrs. White that something must be done or he would bleed to death. We sent the servant to the drug store, got sticking plaster, and washed off the blood to see where he was cut and found five wounds, and as she would wipe off the blood I would draw the wounds together with sticking plaster. In the morning the doctor came, examined him, and found the wounds were not dangerous, and said we had done what was necessary. He got well in a few weeks, but his face was badly scarred, and as long as we stayed at the hotel they did all they could for our comfort, for they felt grateful for my help in their hour of need.

CHAPTER SIX

☆ ☆ ☆ ☆

A few weeks after that I was sitting in my room and a gentleman was announced. I looked up, and who should I see but Capt. St. Clair Morgan?

I said: "My old boy, I am so glad to see you, where did you come from?"

He said: "I came down from the front to get my boys some shoes; they are almost barefooted."

We had a long talk. He said he believed his company was the bravest one in the whole army. He had raised a company of Irish in Nashville, and it did his heart good to see the devotion of these men to him. He said he believed any one of them would die for him. After talking for some time, he bade me good-bye; said he had to hurry to accomplish his business.

The next morning I took the children, as it was my custom, on the front porch to see the cars pass. I saw St. Clair on the train loaded down with shoes. He had strings around his neck and on his arms, and he looked like a bundle of shoes. He was remarkably handsome, and in the strength of his young manhood he was a pleasant picture to look upon. He said in a stentorian voice, "Cousin, I got my shoes for my boys;" and waving a farewell, he was soon lost to view. It was the last time I ever saw him.

By this time there were more fights, and the wounded came down in numbers. I went to the hospitals almost every day, always fearing I would find some of our Nashville boys among the wounded. The ladies of Marietta, and we "refugees," as we were called, did all in our power for the poor boys. I went to the hospital one day to take some delicacies, and as I passed in I was attracted by what I thought the handsomest face I had ever seen. I stopped and spoke to its owner. He looked fresh and ruddy and so young. He had beautiful, laughing brown eyes, and to look at him one would think he was in perfect health. He tried to be cheerful and bright, and seemed anxious to talk. I asked him where he was wounded, and he answered: "Shot through the knee, and the doctor says he fears he will have to amputate my leg; and," he continued, "if they do cut it off, it will almost kill mother and father." I asked him where they lived, and he said in Mississippi. He told me in the conversation that he was an only child; was just twenty-three, and before he enlisted he had entered on the practice of law, after having received an education at Harvard or Yale – I have forgotten which – and said his name was Lieut. Nelson. I learned enough to know he was a mother's darling.

I stayed with him sometime and felt loath to leave him, but told him I would come again soon. He said: "Please come: I feel so lonely and wretched." I felt anxious about him and went back early in the morning: and saw from his face that he had suffered greatly in the night. He told me they had decided to amputate his leg at 12 o'clock that day. I could hardly keep the tears back to see the look of despair on his face when he told me he was afraid he would die, and seemed always to be thinking of the agony it would give his beloved parents, and said: "What will they do without me!" He seemed deeply affected, and I tried to speak words of comfort to him, but I felt faint at heart. I went home, and waited until 4 o'clock, that beautiful face haunting me every moment. I put on my bonnet and hurried to see him, and found the operation had been performed. And O, such a change! He looked haggard and pale, his pulse beating rapidly and breathing with difficulty. He knew me, pressed my hand and held it for some time. I tried in every way to make him feel that he was not alone; that a sympathetic friend was by his side, and he seemed much gratified. I told him to look to God for help; that he alone could save. He listened eagerly, and when I had finished said: "Amen." And in a few minutes he lost consciousness, and I saw he was sinking rapidly. I thought of that poor father and mother so far away, who would never look on the face of their beautiful soldier boy again, and my heart went out in loving sympathy to her as only a mother's heart can. I stayed as long as I could with him, and went weeping home. He died at 8 o'clock that night, and the next day he was gently lowered in a soldier's grave, where he will rest until the trumpet shall sound at that great and final day.

After that many sad scenes were witnessed among the sick and wounded. I read every day in the *Chattanooga Daily Rebel* the list of killed and wounded, and trembled as I did so, fearing some one dear to us would be among them.

Col. Randal McGavock

CHAPTER SEVEN

☆　☆　☆　☆

I corresponded with friends and relatives, constantly hoping to have news from dear ones exposed to danger. One day I received a letter from Richmond, Va., from Mary Valentine, a cousin of mine, telling me that my nephew, Felix Hicks, was with her and was quite a hero, as he had been in a Northern prison for some time. He, with many others, had been captured in one of the battles – I forget which one, for I write from memory – and had been in close confinement, so when an exchange of prisoners was proposed there was great rejoicing. After our boys had boarded a vessel and started to meet the prisoners to be exchanged they found out there was some trouble at Washington about it and no more exchanges would be made then. The boys were turned back to wait results. They were furious, and went to work to make plans for escape. It was agreed that at a given signal they were to seize the guards, disarm and secure them, and make the pilot and engineer do the rest. There were quite a number of prisoners on board. They succeeded in their plans, and by threats and intimidations made the pilot and engineer take them near Norfolk and land them.

They made their way to the swamps and stayed

there two or three days, living on anything they could beg or find to eat. The Federals heard of their escape, and shelled the woods in every direction. After staying together for several days, they thought it best to separate and try to make their way back to the army. So they started, each one looking out for himself. Felix traveled at night until he thought it safe to appear in daylight. He made his way to Richmond, and when he got to Mr. Valentine's he was ragged, dirty, foot-sore, and nearly exhausted. The girls took him in hand and soon had him provided with new clothes and kept him until he was able to travel. He then started to Marietta to see us and stay a little while before rejoining his command. We felt proud of our beardless boy, and enjoyed every minute of his stay with us. The young people all had merry times together. Felix had a fine voice, and he regaled us with many beautiful songs, some he learned in prison. But the sad time came when he had to leave us and return to his regiment, which was then in Mississippi. The next day Col. Randal McGavock came to say good-bye. He looked so bright and hopeful and every inch a soldier. He too went to Mississippi.

Several weeks after this I received a letter from Felix, saying: "After a few more fights Gen. Forrest says that he will give me a furlough of ten days, and I will come to see you all. I can hardly wait, but must exercise patience." We looked anxiously forward to the time when we would see him again. It seemed almost like one of my children coming, and in our exile we felt that these bonds of affection were strengthened. But instead of the visit I received a letter from Capt. Matt Pilcher saying: "Felix was killed today, gallantly fighting for his country. A braver boy I never saw. How my heart goes out to his father and mother, for he was their idol! We are paying dearly for our liberty in giving up so many noble boys."

The next sad news was that Col. Randle McGavock was killed, valiantly fighting near Raymond, Miss.; also Capt. Tom Cooke. My heart sank in gloom, and I asked God for help in these dark hours. These were trying times, and I hope never to see the like again.

News came that preparations were being made to fight at Chickamauga. I knew most of the Calvary would be there. Gen. John T. Morgan's command and Wheeler-'s Division had already gone up. My husband was with the cavalry in his brother's command, and I felt miserable. The battle was fought, and such slaughter and carnage was fearful to relate. Both sides suffered terribly. I scarcely ate or slept, and the suspense was maddening. The intelligence came that Capt. Jackson was killed. We felt this loss deeply, for we were greatly attached to him. He had won our hearts by his gentlemanly bearing, and he was so handsome and brave. His brother, Col. Jackson, was at Marietta on parole, having been captured at Vicksburg when that place surrendered. He and many others were waiting to be exchanged, and were in camp near Marietta. Col. Atkinson and himself went up to get the captain's remains to bury in Marietta. After hunting over the field, they found the poor fellow lying on a blanket with straw under his head; badly wounded, but still alive. They took him to Ringgold; but he was exhausted from loss of blood, and they had no time to attend to his wounds. He never rallied, but died in a few hours after getting him there. They brought his body to Marietta and buried him. Since the close of the war his remains have been removed to Nashville, and now rest at the "Hermitage," near Gen. Andrew Jackson's tomb.

The next day my nurse came up and said a wounded soldier was in the parlor on a cot, and wanted to see me. I wondered who it was, and hurried down, and found Gen. Gregg, of Texas, in a bad condition. He had his face and head bandaged, and seemed in great pain, but he told me he wanted to see me to tell me about Capt. St. Clair Morgan's death.

He said: "He was my devoted friend. I loved him and he was brave to recklessness. He was a friend of my boyhood days, and in the war we were much together. In one of our engagements, on making a terrific charge, Capt. St. Clair was galloping on ahead of me, cheering as he went. And as we came back from the charge I saw a form I thought I knew. Hurriedly jumping down, I raised up the head and saw it was my dear friend. A bullet had entered his forehead and gone through his brain. He died with his face to the foe. He was as brave and daring as any man I ever saw, and had a heart as tender as any woman's."

I felt greatly shocked, for it had been but a short time before that when I saw him, so bright and handsome, with his load of shoes on his way to make his boys comfortable. Now he was still in death, waiting to be placed in a soldier's grave in a strange place.

CHAPTER EIGHT

☆ ☆ ☆ ☆

We were standing one day on the portico watching for the cars to come in, and as the train stopped I saw an aged couple alight, and come feebly up the steps; and just then some friend greeted me. I heard some one say: "Is this Mrs. Morgan?" I said: "Yes." She threw her arms around my neck and wept as though her heart would break, and said, "I am Capt. Jackson's mother, and this is his father," pointing to a venerable-looking old gentleman.

I took them to my room, and after she composed herself, she told me, in a trembling voice, that Capt. Jackson had written to them of his being wounded and the kind friends he had met. They had tried and tried to get a pass to come out to see him, and at last succeeded. They started from the "Hermitage" in a buggy, had their trunk stolen, and after many difficulties got to Cartersvill e, and there learned that their son had been killed and buried at Marietta. They felt that they must come on and hear all they could about their darling boy. I told them all about his sojourn with us, and sent word to Col. and Mrs. Atkinson that they had arrived; and in a little while the colonel's carriage was at the door, and they were soon conveyed to Mrs. Atkinson's residence.

I can never forget Mr. and Mrs. Jackson. She had a sweet, resigned face, and, for an old lady, was beautiful. And he was a dignified, venerable-looking man. They are indelibly impressed on my mind.

She told me she was born in the North, but was devoted to the South, and the dearest treasure of her heart had died battling for its rights. After spending several days in Marietta, and learning all they could of the death of their boy, they came to bid us good-bye. Ah! how my heart went out in sympathy to those weary old pilgrims whom we would never see again until we meet around our Father's throne. We can teach our children to venerate this noble pair, and to love and admire their brave son, who died defending his country.

We were watching and waiting to hear news from other loved ones. We had those who were very dear to us in the cavalry. We heard of them destroying a long train of wagons for the enemy. Then again, they would be miles away, giving them trouble in another direction, and it seemed they were everywhere, watching to see where they could strike a decisive blow. Exciting events were occurring every hour, rumors of fights and news of friends killed or wounded.

One morning a paper was handed to me stating that a terrific fight had taken place, near Farmington, Tenn., between four thousand Confederate cavalry and six thousand Federals. Many were killed and wounded, and among the number was Irby Morgan, of Nashville, mortally wounded. I was almost frantic with grief. My anxiety was terrible.

In a few hours Lieut. Minot, of Gen. John T. Morgan's command, came in a buggy, sent by Mr. Morgan, to tell me to hurry to him. He was on Sand Mountain, and was badly wounded, but alive. The lieutenant told me they had a severe fight, and Capt. Allen, of Mr. Morgan's company, was shot down, and so disabled he could not move. He begged Mr. Morgan not to leave him, and said that he would rather die than be taken prisoner. So Mr. Morgan ran back and was endeavoring to support the captain off the field. Encumbered with his heavy weight, besides his pistol, musket, and cartridge box, his movements were slow. He had gone only a short distance, when he felt a stinging pain in his side, and found the Yankees had discovered his design, and were firing on him from all sides, and a ball struck him in his right hip. It was a miracle he was not killed. He had just reached some cedar trees when he received the wound, but in his excitement he did not think he was much hurt. When he got under cover, he looked down and found the blood gushing out of the top of his cavalry boot, and said to Capt. Allen: "Old fellow, I feel faint, I will have to lay you down, I can't struggle any farther." He laid him down as best he could, and some one saw him and carried him beyond danger of the enemy.

Mr. Morgan had tied his horse near where he attempted to save the captain, so after he was wounded he crawled to his horse, and led the faithful steed along until he got to the surgeon's stand. Then he fainted from loss of blood. His brother got his surgeons to take charge of him. They laid him across some logs, examined his wound, and found his hip shattered and the ball lodged near his spine. They probed and probed, but could not get it out. By that time he was in a dead faint, and they thought they could never bring him to life again. But after using restoratives he opened his eyes. After consultation they decided the ball could not be removed without injuring the spine. His brother put him on a horse and got Mr. Jim Copeland, of Nashville, and Lieuts. Minot and Hyat to ride on each side of him, he being in the center of the column. When he got to Cornersville, an old friend let him have a buggy and harness. They made it secure with ropes and strings, and then got a pillow and put him in the buggy. He could not sit down, so had to kneel on the pillow which was placed in the foot of the conveyance and hold on to the dashboard to steady himself. And when too weary of this position, he would be turned and would rest his head on the seat.

The horse became frightened at something and began to rear and plunge and kick. Mr. Morgan, seeing the danger he was in, crawled up on the seat. The horse gave another plunge, and he went over the back of the buggy. Fortunately, he had presence of mind enough to roll over into a ditch, and the cavalry did not trample him to death. His companions found him and took him into a cornfield, made a fire and kept him as comfortable as possible until morning, when they started for the Tennessee River. He had a horror of being taken prisoner, and would endure any pain to go on with the boys.

They finally got to Sand Mountain, where he met Mr. Jordan, who kept a public house. He was left there until I was sent for, but had every attention and much kindness shown him. After getting settled and feeling happy that he was out of the way of the Federals, he sent Lieut. Minot for me.

I had an infant only a few weeks old, but Dr. Steward told me to go: that I would be better off than to remain in the excited state I was in. I sent for his old father, got a trusty nurse; and when Mr. and Mrs. Tom Marshall heard of it, they came from Cartersville and took charge of my children at the hotel. Several of my friends, among them Rev. John Bryson, went with me to Rome. Then I got a wagon, and in all traveled two hundred and fifty miles.

I found Mr. Morgan terribly wounded, pieces of bone working out, and pieces of his clothing that the ball had carried in worked out too. He also had a raging fever. I watched anxiously day and night for several weeks. One morning he said: "Cheer up. I believe I shall yet pull through, but it was a narrow escape." He gradually grew better; and when I knew all danger was over, it occurred to me that cover for our beds was scarce and hard to get, so I determined to hunt around among the mountain women, and see if I could not buy some homemade worsted counterpanes and blankets. I got some at twenty-five dollars apiece, and they did good service afterward.

We stayed at Mr. Jordan's six weeks, and then decided to travel slowly until we reached Marietta. We got a wagon and put a feather bed in it, and made the horses almost walk until we got to Gadsden, and stopped there to rest, for Mr. Morgan was very weak and greatly fatigued with the trip. We spent the night, and in the morning he was much better.

There was a party of persons going out to see Black Creek Falls, and he insisted that I should go too, as I would never have the opportunity again. So I went, and enjoyed it so much. I was delighted with the view. Black and Clear Creeks unite several miles above the falls, and empty over a precipice of eighty feet. As the sun throws its bright rays on the torrent as it dashes over the falls, it is a grand sight. Under the falls there was a platform erected, and I learned that Wheeler's cavalry had had a dance there a few nights before. From the number of peanut hulls I saw they must have had a jolly time with the country girls. After feasting our eyes on the grand scenery, we went back, and all decided we had been repaid for our trip. The next morning we started for Marietta, and felt almost as if we were going home, for we had so many kind friends there, and we had many to welcome us back. Gen. Bate hobbled out on his poor shattered leg, and his face beamed with pleasure at seeing his old friends again. We found our children well, and all charmed with our dear, faithful friends, Mr. and Mrs. Marshall, for their unremitting kindness to them during our absence.

CHAPTER NINE

☆　☆　☆　☆

News came that Gen. Streight intended to make a raid on Georgia, and great apprehension was felt as to the result. The next report was that Gen. Forrest, with three hundred and fifty men, had, with a ruse, captured seventeen hundred Yankees. We learned of the brave girl who jumped on behind Gen. Forrest on horseback, and went to show him the ford of the river where his soldiers could cross; how he arranged his men in companies, making it appear that soldiers were advancing from every direction, so that Gen. Streight thought he was surrounded with great numbers. Gen. Forrest gave him a certain time to surrender or he would open his batteries on them. They did surrender; and when they learned the small force that had captured them, they were greatly chagrined and morti-fied. We heard that they were to be taken to prison at Andersonville. I felt sad to hear it; for although we were delighted at the brave daring of our much-loved general, we had heard such terrible accounts from our boys in Northern prisons, of suffering and privations, half fed and clad, with sickness and often death, suffering from the rigors of a Northern climate. I thought, "With everything North to eat and wear, if our boys suffer so, what can we do with our limited means to render prisoners comfortable?" and I wished them back with their friends. We were more than willing to provide for them, but what did we have, shut in from the whole world, and most of the men in the army? But we gave our prisoners the best we had, and were always more than willing to exchange.

My servant came up one morning and said: "Gen. Forrest and Mr. George W. Jones wish to see you." I hurried down, and was delighted to meet them; and as Gen. Forrest's wonderful capture was the theme of every fireside, it was doubly interesting to listen to him narrate his wonderful maneuvers, for it would give me something to always remember and repeat with pride. He went into detail, and gave to me an accurate account of the encounter, and I found the report to be pretty correct. I told him what he already knew, how proud we all felt of him, and asked him many questions on the situation of the South. I asked him if he considered this his most brilliant achievement, and he said: "No. The raid I made in Murfreesboro where I captured so many in town and the courthouse, I consider the brightest feather in my cap." He went on to tell me that in Murfreesboro, in July, 1862, he captured the whole garrison: eighteen hundred men, six hundred head of horses and mules, forty wagons, six ambulances, four pieces of artillery, and twelve hundred stand of small arms. This was done by a force equal in numbers to the Federals captured. "The military stores taken by me in this affair were valued at $1,000,000." When I looked into his calm face and clear gray eyes I could hardly realize the pent up force that was smoldering there. But woe to the coward or straggler! They had better meet the enemy than to encounter him.

After he left I had quite a levee, for the ladies

came in troops to hear what their brave chieftain had to say. You can't imagine in this day how excited and enthusiastic the women became. The news of victory was like an electric spark that set us all on fire.

Our Nashville friends were now all scattered in every direction, and when we would get letters, which were few and far between, we would send them all around to the rest. We corresponded with a good many of our soldier boys, and we were often enabled to send them news of their friends. I have many of these letters now, and they are precious relics.

My husband received a letter from Dr. McTyeire, from Butler Lodge, Ala., where he was with his family. He wrote: "John and myself expect to raise a large lot of cowpeas. Let Bob come down, and I will teach him to plow. We hope we will succeed, for this will be my chief dependence for a living. Little did I think when my father died, and a few old servants cared for the place, that I would ever feel thankful to have it for a retreat for my family. My wife and children are bearing their exile so cheerfully."

He told me that he was the only white man left in the neighborhood, as all the others were in the army, and he spent his time preaching and looking after the widows and children, and working on his farm. We received letters from Dr. Summers, Dr. A. L. P. Green, Col. Samuel D. Morgan, Gen. John H. Morgan, and many others. I have them now, and often take them out and read them to my children and grandchildren. But I am digressing.

Gen. John Hunt Morgan

CHAPTER TEN

☆ ☆ ☆ ☆

Mr. Morgan was still weak, suffering from his wounds. He was put on the retired list. The crowd was surging in our direction, the hotels were crowded with gamblers and bad characters, drinking, carousing, coming and going. Food was getting scarcer and cooking worse. To sum it up, confusion reigned. One day Col. John Savage came to me and said they had changed the name of the hotel. I asked him the new name, and he said: "H—l and hash house, instead of Kennesaw Hotel." I told him that was a fearful name, but he went off laughing heartily.

The time had come when we had to make a change. Houses were hard to get; we were in a sad dilemma; we did not know what to do. Fortunately, we heard of a house for sale, furnished complete throughout, everything to be sold. It was a convenient place, with large rooms and a good many of them. We were pleased with it, so bought and moved into it at once, as the family occupying it were anxious to go South. In a short time Col. Samuel D. Morgan heard of our move, and wrote to me to try to get a house near us, as he was anxious to get his family together. After many trials we succeeded in getting a house next to us, the Episcopal church intervening. He wrote to Dr. Robert Williams and family, and with his granddaughters, the Misses Cheney, they came to Marietta and went to housekeeping.

About that time the contents of the trunk I brought from Nashville were nearly exhausted, and it was almost an impossibility to get goods for clothing. Some ran the blockade and got goods from Memphis and some of the Atlantic ports, but they were the fortunate few that succeeded. The girls needed clothes and had to have them, so I got a bolt of hickory stripe made by our factories. I will describe it for the benefit of the girls of to-day: It was pin-striped, blue and white, made of fine thread, heavier than gingham. I made a dress each for my two girls and two nieces. The style of make was a yoke, full sleeves, sash of the same, and four folds stitched on the bottom of the skirts. Two of the dresses were headed at the top of the fold with red and two with white cord, and when they were done I thought them beautiful.

The girls decked out in them and felt so independent in their Southern-woven dresses, and proud too that they were Southern girls. These were among their best dresses, and as they were satisfied and pleased, I was happy to see them contented. The next serious question was where to get food, as our family was very large and the house crowded all the time with friends; so our supplies had to be considerable, and it gave us much cause for worry. There were an old gentleman and lady of Northern birth who had lived there for many years, and had shown us much kindness. They had a nice place near town, and raised quantities of vegetables and had nice fruits, and they were thoughtful and kind, often sending us baskets of fresh vegetables, honey, and fruits. We persuaded them to sell us everything we needed in that line.

We always had a cordial welcome to their home, and many nice dinners we have eaten with them. We needed meats and many things the old gentleman couldn't supply, so Mr. Morgan sent for him and got him to consent to go up and down the road to get supplies. He got us flour, two barrels of molasses, cowpeas, hams, meal, and many other necessaries. Besides these articles, he bought beef cattle that were poor, and Mr. Morgan got Joe, my faithful servant boy, to boil bran, cowpeas, and corn together and give them all they could eat, and we soon had a lot of fine beeves to kill. I had a good receipt for corning beef, and I succeeded finely in keeping it, and we made many a soldier boy's heart glad by dividing with him. We raised chickens, or attempted to do so, and we had a time, as our place was near the depot. We were fortunate enough to get a good cow, had a little garden, and some fig trees were on the place which bore an abundance of luscious fruit. This was a new sight to us, fig trees bearing, but we soon learned to think them great delicacies. We considered ourselves very fortunate in having so many of the necessaries of life, and it made us happy to divide with those who couldn't get these things. Meat was a great item in housekeeping and it was hard to get, as the army consumed so much.

In a short while Col. Samuel D. Morgan got a letter from John H. Morgan, saying: "I will soon be married to Miss Mattie Ready, of Murfreesboro, Tenn." We had had no intimation of any such thing, and were greatly surprised to hear it. When Gen. Basil Duke and he came to see us on Lookout Mountain, I thought he was too much absorbed in the war to think of marrying; but he did take unto himself a wife, and came down to Marietta to see us all, his uncle's family and ours. We were delighted to see him again, for he had by his bravery, dash, and brilliant achievements distinguished himself, and we felt he was a deserved hero, and we delighted in honoring him. When he came with his pretty young wife, we thought a handsomer couple could not be found. He had a magnificent figure, was remarkably handsome, and was every inch a soldier. He was kind and pleasant to every one he met, and I think had more personal magnetism than any one I ever knew. The citizens toasted and feasted them and made their ten days' stay delightful.

We had then a little baby six months old, named Cornelia Hunt, the middle name for him. He loved children, but was especially fond of this little curly-headed one that bore his name, and would always call for her when he came. During their stay in Marietta, they rode frequently on horseback, and many times we would watch them with interest and think how distinguished they looked. He often talked to us about the war, and one night we all gathered around him, the children all excitement, wanting to catch every word, and asked him to tell us of some of his daring deeds. He related many incidents that had occurred since he started out, but after a lapse of thirty years many of them have escaped my memory. But one incident I recall. He said he heard a long train would leave Louisville on a certain day filled with clothes for the soldiers and army stores of all kinds and in large quantities. He made a dash into Kentucky, and by traveling day and night met the train just beyond Mammoth Cave. His daring soldiers dashed up and stopped the train. He said it was the longest one he ever saw, not only filled with army stores, but a great many ladies going to Nashville, some to join their husbands and others to meet their sweethearts, for the Federals were having a nice time in

Nashville. When the train was drawn up, he said he never saw such consternation depicted on faces. One old lady ran up to him and begged him not to kill her; told him to take all she had, but spare her life. He remarked that it made him feel embarrassed to be regarded as a murderer of helpless women and children – a man who had always been proverbial for his gallantry to ladies; but such horrible tales had been told about him that they were prepared to meet a brigand, and they regarded him as a monster in human guise. He said his soldiers and himself ran from car to car and escorted the women and children out, placed them where they would be out of danger, and then went to work to destroy and burn up everything, he taking time to run out and reassure the ladies that they should not be hurt. Some of them begged him piteously for their trunks, but he told them he was sorry that his time was too limited to show them such courtesies. Some laughed at the ludicrous position they were in, and others rained down imprecations on his head. The soldiers made a complete wreck of everything, and with a military salute and profound bow bade the ladies farewell, jumped on their horses, and were gone. That train was a great loss to the Federals, and as such large stores of clothes and army supplies were burned, it retarded their progress for several days.

His delightful visit was as drawing to an end, he was much impressed with the kindness shown him by all, and said his visit would not be soon forgotten. He came to say good-bye to us, and I made him promise to keep us posted as to his movements, and he said he would send us *Videttes* from every point he made a raid. This little paper was edited by Major Gano, of his command just a small sheet, inferior paper, and published hastily, but gave the welcome news of his movements. I have some of them now; but they are old, ragged, and worn. The last one we got was from Hartsville, Tenn., telling of his fight and captures there. Not long after that he was captured by the Federals and taken to a Northern prison, and as all are familiar with his capture I will not recount it, but a letter written to his uncle describing his feelings and thoughts while imprisoned thrilled us at the time.

CHAPTER ELEVEN

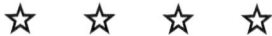

☆ ☆ ☆ ☆

John H. Morgan went on to tell his different plans for escape. He described the dogs in the prison yard, and how ferocious they were, and knew he would have to pass these brutes to get out of the inclosure. And many hours he would roll from side to side on his cot, and try to think of some way to get them off his track; but it seemed that all schemes failed. He said he felt that to have gotten them out of his way he would have eaten them. He made his escape from prison one dark night when the rain was pouring down in torrents, and succeeded in crawling by the guard, hardly breathing until all danger was past.

After his death a good many of his command were stationed near Marietta with Wheeler's Division. They would come in often to see us. Many of them I had met on Lookout Mountain. Among them were Drs. Joe and Charlie Tidings, surgeons in Morgan's command. They were very kind to us, and gave me a case of medicines, with instructions how to use them in case of emergency, for physicians were so much in demand, caring for the sick and wounded, that it was often with difficulty that they could be found when needed. They were kind and attentive to Mr. Morgan in his weakened condition. The ball in his side could not be removed, and it gave him continual pain, pressing against his spine. The surgeons told him that after awhile a sack would gradually form around the ball, but not to entertain any hope that it could ever be extracted. He is now an old man, many long years have elapsed since those stirring and sorrowful times, and the ball is often still a reminder of those days of strife and bloodshed.

I had so many cares now. I could not go to the hospitals as often as I wished, but whenever I could find time I would prepare waiters of delicacies, and the girls would help me take them. They would wait at the doors and I would go through and distribute them to the poor, desolate, homesick boys, and my heart would bound with pleasure to see the grateful look of appreciation on their poor, sunken faces; and they would tell me how good everything tasted after eating so much old light bread and soup. Capt. Jim Barnes and Capt. Ed Douglass, of Nashville, came from East Tennessee with rheumatism, and stayed with me two months, until they got well enough to join their commands.

The army was still falling back and fighting almost all the time, for they contested every foot of ground from Dalton to Atlanta, though against overwhelming numbers. Such deeds of bravery and valor were never surpassed; but were shared by Wheeler, Cheatham, Dibrell, Morgan, and indeed all, for it would be hard to discriminate, they all fought so bravely.

I heard that Col. Terry Cahal, one of our Nashville boys, was badly wounded. They were in a fight, and he leaped over the fortifications and wrested the colors from the enemy, and in his effort to get back was shot. I had him brought to my home, where I could watch him. He was telling me of the fight with great exultation, and said that he did not mind being hurt to get their colors. His wound was not as serious as it was at first thought to be. He was considered brave and daring almost to recklessness.

Marietta, being so near the army was now crowded all the time, and our house filled to overflowing. It was very elastic, and we could always find room for one more. One night we had as guests Gen. John M. Bright, Gov. Neil S. Brown, Judge Marchbanks, Dr. C.D. Elliott, Rev. John Bryson, Col. Robinson, Col. Terry Cahal, and Dr. John B. McFerrin. We had two mattresses on most of the beds, so we would take one off of each and spread them around in different rooms, parlor included. Our family was large, so with these guests added it looked like a small hotel. I had to put Dr. McFerrin in the bed with a very fleshy man, and expressed my regrets, but he said: "Don't worry, sister, for this is good sleeping; better than I have been used to, for I have been lying on the ground in camp with the boys."

The all-absorbing theme was the removal of Gen. Joe Johnston. Many thought that President Davis had committed the error of his life, for Gen. Johnston had only to command and the soldiers obeyed, never questioning a move, for they had implicit confidence in him. And the soldiers would often say: "What old Joe does is all right. He knows what he is about." With Gen. Hood they had some fears; but their ardor for the cause was so great that they did not stop to cavil, but rushed with impetuosity to accomplish all they were ordered to do. They often said, afterward: "If old Joe had been left in command, Gen. Sherman would never have got to the ocean." President Davis was terribly censured, but his conduct since then for thirty years has refuted all charges and calumny imputed to him at the time. When I think of that grand character, sometimes seeming almost isolated, censured by the South for what they conceived an error of judgment, and calumniated all over the North, I wonder that that proud spirit of that weak body did not succumb. But he was so deeply imbued with the idea of sovereignty of the States that he died battling for what he conceived to be the bulwark of the South, these rights.

Well, many changes were taking place on all sides. The school our girls had attended, taught by Mr. Benedict, was given up, and we were greatly worried as to where we would send them. Mr. Jesse Thomas, of Nashville, came to Marietta; and knowing how competent Miss Kate Thomas was as a teacher, we begged her to take a class. She timidly shrank from anything of the kind, but after a good deal of persuasion we got her to consent to open a school. Col. Samuel D. Morgan sent his granddaughters, Mr. Lytton his girls, four went from our home, and from the ladies of Marietta she had many applications. Many a glad mother had reason to thank Miss Kate for the training of her daughters in gentle, ladylike deportment, and classic and text-book knowledge.

CHAPTER TWELVE

☆ ☆ ☆ ☆

We would have daily visits from some of our boys.
Hardly a day would pass but what we would see some
familiar face. Gens. Cheatham and Bate, Capts. Joe Phil-
lips and Van McIver, Maj. James W. Thomas, Lieut.
George Lytton, Capt. Matt Pilcher, Mr. Jim Buckner,
Capts. James Cooper, Capt. John Morton, Collins Bright,
and many others too numerous to mention. Gen. Frank
Cheatham, "Our Frank," as the boys called him, would run
in occasionally. He was always jolly, but often looked
weather beaten, with faded clothes and bronzed face. The
boys would say: "We will go anywhere old Frank orders
us, even were it in the cannon's mouth." He reminded me
of an old Roman soldier, so dignified when commanding
his troops; but when not on duty, he was a genial compan-
ion. We felt proud of our Tennessee boys, but had an
especially tender place for the "Rock City Guards," as
they were boys we had known all our lives; but all knew
that they had a welcome at our home, and whenever they
could get leave of absence for a few days, would slip
down to Marietta, and we would spend happy hours
together, and many a little entertainment the girls would
get up for their pleasure, and such hunting of clothes and

decking out was right laughable. My husband's wardrobe was drawn on until he could sometimes scarcely find a change of clothes, white shirts particularly, and handkerchiefs. Pieces of ribbon and anything were used for cravats; but the boys had a merry time, anyway, and old Marietta would resound with their enthusiastic songs: "Bonnie Blue Flag," "Dixie," "My Maryland," and many others I have forgotten. They would often wind up with "Home, Sweet Home," and the tears would gather in their eyes. They would have for refreshments, popcorn, sorghum candy, gooberpeas, and sometimes cake, and all kinds of fruits. How they would enjoy it, after eating hard bread and bacon, and sometimes beans and cowpeas for days! When they would start back, I would fill their canteens with buttermilk and sorghum molasses, give them a piece of corned beef and some beaten biscuit, and they would feel rich and happy.

Our old friend, Gen. John M. Bright, had a son not quite fourteen years old, who gave him great uneasiness. He was well grown for his age, looked older than he was; and as his brothers were in the army, he was anxious to go too, but his father thought it best for him to stay in Lincoln County with his family. But news came that John Massey, a splendid young man, and others, of Fayetteville, had been shot by order of a Federal general for bushwhacking. John was of an impetuous disposition, and his father determined to get him out of the lines, for fear he would be killed. He finally succeeded, and sent him to Chapel Hill, N.C., to school, paid his tuition in advance, and in talking to me about him congratulated himself on the good arrangements he had made for him, and that a great trouble had been lifted off him. After a few weeks Johnny appeared at my door, carpetbag in hand, greeted me, and was overjoyed to see us. I in return was delighted to see him, for I loved him very dearly. His mother had been one of my cherished friends for years.

I expressed great surprise, and asked him how he got here. He said: "Well, Aunt Julia, I couldn't study, and I worried and worried the teacher until he gave my money back. If he had not done it, I would have run off, for I intend to join the army."

He opened his valise and commenced pulling out clothes, and said: "See what I have brought you all." He had a thin summer coat for Mr. Morgan, and a handsome meerschaum pipe, and something for the children and myself, and he presented them with a beaming face.

I told him that I was very sorry he had spent his money. "Your father was here last week and told me that his family were having a hard time at home in the lines, and needed that money."

He looked very sorrowful for a few minutes, but in a little while after I heard his merry laugh with the children, and I went in and asked him what he intended to do. He said that in a few days he intended to go up to the army, but I knew that his father would not consent to it for a moment, for he was entirely too young. I consulted Mr. Morgan, and we decided that he should not go, and told him so, and also informed him that he had to start to school, which he reluctantly consented to do.

The next morning we encountered him, and we had a merry time watching John to keep him from running off. His father was urging him all the time to stay and try to improve his time, and insisted on us controlling him as we would our own boy. I had my seven children, two nieces, and John, making ten young people in all, and my hands and heart were full of anxieties and cares. My husband was still feeble. He hobbled around on crutches, and gave me all the assistance he could in managing the children and household.

Joe, my faithful servant, worked my garden, and we had a quantity of nice, fresh vegetables, plenty of milk and butter, meat, flour, and so on; but our soap gave out, and we could not buy it. We were in a dilemma – war times, and no soap. A friend of my husband told him that they had at the commissary department a large lot of refuse grease, and said that if we would send for it we could have it. So we did send, and got the grease, and also a quantity of wood ashes from friends. I called Joe up, and asked him if he could make an old fashioned lye hopper. So we went to work, run the lye down, and began on our soap. In a few days we had four barrels of fine lye soap, but my eyes were nearly smoked out. I was proud of my success, and made enough to last me till the close of the war.

We often wondered that we had nothing stolen, as there were so many coming and going all the time, colored and white. I will mention a fact that astonished every one. The morning I left Nashville I hastily gathered up six or seven dozen knives, forks, and spoons, small and large, with my name on them. I used them constantly in the house and kitchen – for I had no others – never losing a single piece, and when I came back to Nashville I brought them all home safely. It was remarkable how little stealing was done, especially in provisions, for so many were on short rations.

I must say that we should never forget the negroes, for they were faithful and industrious, and seemed to face their responsibilities. Many said to me: "De las' promise I made old master was, I would take good care of missus and de chilluns." And faithfully did they keep their promise. When news would come that an old or young master was killed, they would weep with the family pure tears of affection. I would hear the old mammies tell of the different ones of the children that they had "nussed," and now they were big soldier boys, and had gone to fight for their country, and in letters these boys would write home there were always messages of love for their "dear old mammy." And when the brave boys gave up their lives and were fortunate enough to be sent home, those black mammies were among the first to show the last tender love and respect for their beloved dead. They were always proud of "our white folks," as they called them, and were ever ready to do their bidding and attend to every want. I do not remember a single act of lawlessness on their part during the war. I have a warm place in my heart for the negroes, and can't help but feel grateful to them for their unremitting fidelity to us during the long struggle.

The army was now falling back slowly but surely, and we would hear of thrilling deeds of daring on the part of our brave boys led by our faithful and chivalrous Gen. Dibrell: making a dash where the enemy least expected them, killing and capturing many. His command were devoted to him. The boys would (different ones) get leave of absence, and would nearly always come down to spend a few days among Nashville friends. It did our hearts good to see them eat. Many, many times when they would be in a hurry to start back I would make them go out and help the girls churn, so they could take their canteens full of fresh buttermilk; and what a frolic they would make of it!

Letters often came asking us to send or buy for them articles of clothing, and particularly shoes, and often they did not fit, but would have to be worn. You must not suppose for a moment that we were the only workers, for many others were doing as much and more than we. But I started out to tell what I saw, heard, and did, and I was kept so busy that I didn't have time to know what others were doing.

The soldiers were the most cheerful persons we would see. They would come with their clothes faded, ragged, and drawn up from rain and exposure until the tops of their socks were showing, and we would never hear a murmur or complaint from them.

One day Neil Brown came in to see us. He looked so weather-beaten that I scarcely recognized him. I gazed at his handsome, bronzed face – only a beardless boy – and thought him the picture of bravery, and he looked as if the word "fail" never entered his vocabulary, although it appeared dark to us. You would see often perfect caricatures among the poor fellows, but if it made them sensitive, they didn't show it. They seemed merry and light-hearted, and I would often look at them and wonder that in the midst of so many uncertainties how they could be bright; for who knew but that before the week was out some of them would be still in death. I could hardly restrain my tears before them, and would often leave them to conceal my emotions. Many of these dear ones I had known from childhood, and in our exile they felt very near to us. With how much pleasure did we contribute to their wants and try to make their stay with us pleasant! And when we would bid them good-bye, it was often their last farewell on earth.

CHAPTER THIRTEEN

☆　☆　☆　☆

I was suffering great apprehension every day about my seven-year-old boy, for fear he would be killed. I had made him an artillery suit, and he would tell every one that he belonged to Capt. John Morton's battery, and he really thought he was a soldier. He had a dozen little boys he would drill, and called them his company. They would march up and down the street, and frequently during the day you could hear "hep, hep," stepping to the music of drums and tin horns, or anything that came handy that they could make a noise with. Sometimes tin pans and sticks would be a substitute for lack of something better. He was a sprightly little fellow, and the soldiers nearly ruined him. He called old and young by their first names – John or Tom, or whatever it might be. I would reprove him, and he would say: "They told me to call them that." It all did very well for awhile, and amused us, but he began to think he was monarch of all he surveyed, and acted accordingly. He would run off from home and I would hear of him riding behind one of the soldiers in one direction, and a little while after he would be seated up beside the driver on an artillery wagon sailing another way. I would send runners to hunt him, would bring him home and punish him; but often the temptation to be with the soldiers would overcome him, and he would start again. He would listen to them talk, and he would tell us marvelous tales. He had no idea of numbers and his hundreds of killed and wounded would swell up into the thousands. To sum it all up, he was fast getting to be a regular newsmonger, and was as well known as any boy in Marietta. He knew persons I had never heard of, and would yell out, "Howdy, Bill," maybe to some settled man, or one with gray hairs. But to top the climax, Mr. Fred Shepherd came leading him in one day, and told me if I didn't want a dead boy I would have to keep him at home. He said: "I just pulled him out from under a car that was oscillating, ready to start. His whole bag of marbles had tumbled out and had rolled under the cars, and he started right after them, and I happened along just in time to save him." It was such a narrow escape that it made me tremble, and I thought: "What shall I do with him?" I was almost in despair. I had whipped him, put him to bed, tied him to a chair, and would often bribe him to be good.

He had quite a contempt for girls, and thought it a great insult to be called like them. So I thought over every mode of punishment, and concluded I would put a hoop skirt on him and a dress with a long train.

I said: "My son, I have tried to have a nice boy, but he is so bad and runs away so much I will have to make a little girl of him." He wailed, but I persisted, and took my chair for the evening and stayed with him. In a short while several persons came up to my room, and he would run behind the door, pulling his train after him. He would stay still for some time, until his curiosity would get the best of him and he would peep out. Some of the ladies got a glimpse of his hoop skirt, and laughed heartily, and asked me what on earth was the matter with the child. I told them I had made a girl of him to keep him at home; that he ran away and behaved so badly. Then he would scream and cry and try to explain, but I persisted; and late in the evening he got so tired of the room he ventured out in the hall to see what was going on among the children, but as soon as he spied them he came flying back and they after him to know what was the matter. But "Sallie," as I called him, got in first, trail and all, and slammed the door and said: "Please, ma'am, take them off, and I will never run off again." It did break him of this troublesome habit of running off, but in after years I had cause to regret it; for the name followed him to Nashville, and more than one fight resulted from his being called by that name. And whenever they did dare to utter that name they would prepare to get out of his way, for rocks would fly in the cause. But after he grew up to manhood the name seemed to have a fascination for him, for his partner for life was called "Sallie."

Gen. Frank Cheatham

CHAPTER FOURTEEN

☆ ☆ ☆ ☆

The lines were tightening each day. Fights occurred constantly below Dalton, the troops stoutly contesting every inch of ground. We would hear startling rumors every hour of the nearness of the enemy. Now and then Gen. Frank Cheatham would run in for an hour or two. We had great confidence in him, and looked up to him as one of our bravest leaders. He was so sympathetic and kind to the boys that they almost idolized him, and the soldiers would often say to me: "Why, old Frank is one of the boys." But in battle they obeyed him implicitly.

As the army was falling back now daily, Mr. Morgan was in great trouble about us; he didn't know whether to send us farther south or to let us remain in Marietta. He had his old father and his sister and family on a little farm living comfortably, and as we were well fixed in Marietta and the children at school, he concluded the best thing to do in the event of the enemy getting to Marietta, was to let us remain quietly in the lines and he would go farther South. In the meanwhile the excitement was getting to fever heat, and as the children shared with the older ones in this terrible nervous strain, they became so excited that study was out of the question. My nieces went out to stay a few days with their mother, never dreaming of any trouble. The enemy were advancing, and soon old Kennesaw resounded with the roar of artillery. We would go out at night and listen to the reverberation of that old mountain, knowing that every shot was the death knell of some dear one. O the tension was fearful! How my heart would go out to our dear boys and the loved ones at home! But all we could do was to bow our heads in prayer and beg God to help us all and sustain us by His grace. Nearer and nearer the sounds would come, the excitement increasing.

I never will forget the day the news came that Gen. Polk was killed. He was greatly beloved by all, not only for his bravery, but for his pure Christian character. The next startling information was that the enemy were in a few miles of the town in overwhelming numbers, and were advancing rapidly. The scene beggared description – the town was almost in a frenzy of excitement. Our house was crowded with soldiers, as the army was almost in the town. The boys begged Mr. Morgan to take us south, and he said he had moved his family so much he didn't see how he could go farther; but that boom, boom, boom got to be every minute, resounding from hilltop to hilltop. We could see the smoke from the firing. O, it was a grand but awful sight! We could do nothing but walk, talk, and wait, feeling that some great calamity was impending. We could hear nothing from Sister Lucy and family, and knew by that time that the enemy were near her house, and we thought of the girls, the old father and daughter in their helpless condition, and we were miserable. We knew the old man could do nothing to protect them, and our hands were equally powerless; we were nearly crazy.

All the information we could glean was that our army was fighting as few ever fought, and falling on all sides. About 11 o'clock we saw an ambulance stop at the gate, and my first thought was that some dear one, wounded or dead, had been brought to us. We ran to see who it was, when sister and girls bounded out, then the old father and three negroes, all in a pitiful condition. Their clothes were muddy, bedraggled, and saturated with water. They told us the Federal batteries were planted so that they swept the house, and shell after shell was sent crashing and shrieking through the house. At intervals they tried to get their precious clothes, and succeeded and tied them up in bundles and then started to run. A shell would burst near them and they would drop their treasures and cry awhile, then at an interval seize them and start running until they got far enough to feel safe from the shells. It commenced raining, and they were in a deplorable condition.

Gen. John T. Morgan, her brother, with his command, had been for several days around and in her house, as she knew many of them; but he had taken part of his troops and had gone around in another direction to meet the enemy, leaving part of his command with Wheeler's Brigade. When they returned to where Wheeler's troops were stationed and heard of the sad plight the family were in, the boys were furious; they believed it premeditated cruelty on the part of the Federals. They jumped on their horses and in the midst of flying shells rode up to where the helpless family were in the woods near their house. The enemy in passing had raided the house, and as they could not carry off the things, had deliberately ripped open feather beds and had the contents flying in every direction; had knocked in the heads of several bar-

rels of molasses and did all the damage they could. After
they left our boys went into the house and saved what
things they thought most essential for the family and that
could be hurriedly moved; brought ambulances enough
to carry the family and what was left of their belongings
to Marietta. Some of the boys laughed and said the last
things they saw were ducks, chickens, and turkeys strug-
gling in molasses and feathers.

After hearing of the treatment they had received,
we were terribly frightened, and begged to be taken farther
south. The soldiers told Mr. Morgan they would help us
in every way to get ready for a hasty departure, so he tele-
graphed a friend in Augusta to get us a place. He succeeded in renting half of a house on the Sand Hills, near
Augusta. After we decided to go there was no time to lose,
so the soldier boys went to work, helped to take down the
beds and furniture, and we got things packed up in a short
time. Maj. Cummings kindly let us have cars enough to
hold our things. Gen. John M. Bright, Col. Terry Cabal,
Capt. Collins Bright, Jim Buckner, and many of the Rock
City Guards came in and went to work. Such a hurry and
confusion there was then, all anxious to see us start. By
this time pandemonium reigned in the streets – soldiers,
wagons, artillery wagons, drivers shouting and hurrying,
and the "tramp, tramp, tramp" was heard in every direction, all falling back as fast as possible, going to Atlanta
to make a stand. We were soon in readiness, all of our
small possessions packed in the cars. Mr. Morgan, his
father and sister with her family, the children and myself,
and our faithful Joe got on the car and started to Atlanta.
On arriving in that city, we were in such a crowd we had
to wait some time before we could push through. Every
little while some kind friend would come in and speak a

word of encouragement and offer to render some assistance. Maj. John Bransford was also among our friends who volunteered his services.

Gen. Joseph Wheeler

CHAPTER FIFTEEN

☆ ☆ ☆ ☆

We were worn out from work and anxiety, and so tired waiting, and were almost famished for water. It was very scarce, as hundreds of soldiers and people from every direction were thirsty too, and were begging for it on all sides. I don't know when I ever felt so gratified in all my life as when old Dr. Hudson, of Nashville, came up with a tin bucket of cool, fresh buttermilk. He told me that he had walked for some time trying to find this milk for the children and myself; had offered to buy it, and finally he succeeded in begging this bucketful. I thought it the most delicious milk that I had ever tasted. We all enjoyed it and thanked the old gentleman most heartily. We looked and wondered how he had squeezed through that surging mass, and felt grateful beyond expression for his kindness. It was indeed the cup of cold water given to the thirsty.

From Atlanta, Mr. Morgan sent his father, sister, and her little children to Alabama, and we started with our family and two nieces to Augusta, and thence to the Sand Hills, a lovely suburb of Augusta, and we were fortunate enough to rent half of a house owned by two sisters, Mrs. Edgar and Miss Carmichael, nieces of Dr. Paul

F. Eve, of Nashville. They gave us a warm welcome to a delightful home. We had five large rooms and were pleasantly situated, and remained with them until the war closed. Mrs. Edgar, sister, and two boys just returned from the Virginia Military Institute occupied the other half of the house. We never had kinder friends than they were, and the friendship has been continued since the war.

In a short time there was a call for ladies, men, boys, and girls to come to the Arsenal to help make cartridges, and as they were needed, the girls from Augusta and the Sand Hills (mine among the number) responded. The girls were patriotic, and didn't shrink from doing anything to help the cause so near to our hearts. They didn't ask, "What can I do?" but, "What must I do?" willing to have work assigned them. They went every day and worked faithfully for several weeks, and for some time after this. They would bring home as a souvenir a cartridge they had helped make, and the patriotic Southern blood burned proudly in their veins as they would tell how faithfully they had labored for their country.

Thus the work at the Arsenal went steadily on, and to increase the interest and hasten the work, they began to pay from fifty cents to $1 a day. The girls were too patriotic to take any money for their services, but the little boys thought that they would make a little money for themselves, and at night on their return they would compare notes and have a big counting, and they thought themselves very rich.

One night I overheard a conversation between Johnny Bright and my little son. He told him that he had saved up $30, and he would show them all what he intended to do with it. And on being pressed to know what he had on hand, said: "I am going to run off and join the army." I walked in and said: "Well, young man, what will your $30 buy? You need shoes and a hat now, and your money won't buy you a pair of shoes" – for by that time the money had depreciated so that everything brought fabulous prices. He looked crestfallen, and did not say anything again for some time about going. I do not give dates of occurrences, for after thirty years, and writing from memory, many facts as well as dates have been forgotten.

A few weeks after my encounter with John Bright we sent our two daughters and two nieces to Eatonton, Ga., to school to Mrs. Jane T.H. Cross, an old Nashville teacher, who had opened a large school there. Other Nashville girls attend the same school, and our girls boarded with Mr. Jesse Thomas's family. A few days after they left, Mr. Allen Washington, wife, and five children came from Marietta, and remained with us until he could secure them a home elsewhere. Mr. Washington was in the government clothing department, and he was kept pretty busy securing clothing for our needy boys. Among others from Nashville who took a prominent part in this department were Maj. V.K. Stephenson, Mr. George O'Bryan, Mr. George Cunningham, and Mr. Tom Massengale. Mr. Washington would run down every few days to spend a day and night with his family, and after several efforts he finally secured them a home. After they left I commenced my work again in the hospitals. I found them crowded with our wounded boys, and more coming in every day. I offered to help in any way I could, and they told me that it was hard work for them to get enough for all to eat, and if I would help prepare food for them it would be a great blessing. So I told them that I would cook two days in each week for the gangrene hospital. They sent me out a number of hams and sacks of flour, and I got Joe to build up a fire under a large kettle I had, and we would boil a number of the hams at once. While they were cooking, we would make up a large lot of beaten biscuit, and the ladies of the Sand Hills were very kind in making frequent donations of delicacies, and the next morning I would start with the nice things, just as happy as I could be to feel that I could minister to the sufferers. Joe would take the express and I the barouche, often well packed, and I would go in and out to help distribute, always looking for our Nashville boys. In these many journeys made, my heart was gladdened when I could see the look of pleasure and gratitude on many pinched and suffering faces. Many bandages did I remove, and would wash and dress the wounds, for the surgeons were so rushed it was impossible to pay the attention that cases really needed. Often letters would have to be written to the absent loved ones at home, some the last love greetings they would ever get from their soldier boys. O the horrors of war! I hope I will never have to pass through such heartrending scenes again. If I could remember all the sad sights I witnessed during the four years I was south, it would fill a large volume, for I was in the midst of it from the time I left Lookout Mountain till the close of the war.

CHAPTER SIXTEEN

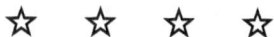

☆　☆　☆　☆

In a few weeks we had a colony of Tennesseeans on the hill. Col. E. W. Cole, Mr. Tom Massengale, Mr. Gerry Pearl, Maj. Cunningham, all with their families, and many others too numerous to mention. We were all kept busy, and it seemed to me that the Southern women thought nothing too difficult to undertake, always feeling that where there was a will there was a way out of all difficulties. I went one day to see Mrs. Col. Cole, who was a big-hearted, thoroughgoing woman, and loyal to her country. On entering the room I heard a peculiar noise, and I asked what it was. She told me it was silkworms feeding; and sure enough there they were, feasting on leaves. She said: "The soldiers, many of them my friends, need silk handkerchiefs, and I have already woven quite a number." And when she showed me the results of her labor, I was astonished.

Things were developing so fast that the crisis seemed almost upon us. We were almost in the throes of death, and fighting desperately was the order of the day. Many more wounded men were brought to Augusta, and among them Capt. Collins Bright. He was badly wounded, gangrene had set in, and he was in a pitiful condition. He sent me word he was there, and I went in immediately to see him. My husband told me before starting that I must use every effort that I could to get permission to bring him home with me, so we could nurse and give him that attention he could not receive at the hospital. Capt. Bright said his destination was another point, but he heard that we were near Augusta, so he begged to be taken there. The officers had given orders that none should be taken to private houses, as many were already scattered in different directions, and some tarried longer than the officials thought necessary. I begged hard and long before I could gain their consent to remove him. Then certain conditions were imposed that I thought rather hard. They were to this effect: That I must come in every morning at 9 o'clock and report his condition. I gladly consented, and with his servant's (Ira) help got him in the carriage and we both started home happy.

I got directions from the doctor what to do, and upon examination found he was wounded above the knee on the underside of his leg, and a large hole was there where the flesh had been shot away. When I looked at the lacerated, angry-looking leg, I felt faint and turned away, but only for a moment, for he was suffering intensely. I went to work, and with Ira's assistance, bathed and dressed it. He suffered agonies, for the leaders in the leg could be plainly seen where the flesh was torn out. He was unable to move himself, and he was weak and feverish. I had to obey orders and be at the hospital not later than 9 o'clock to report his condition. I went for a week and found it exceedingly irksome, and began to feel that it was a farce. One morning I found quite a number of young doctors in the office, looking gay and jolly. They were laughing and talking, and seemed to be having a good time. I said:

"Gentlemen, I want to see Dr. Paul F. Eve." They told me that he was not in, and didn't know where he could be found, as he was going all the time from one hospital to another. I said to them that if I could see him I knew he would put a stop to all this foolishness, coming to report every day that my soldier had not run off, when he was too weak to turn in his bed. They laughed and said: "Madam, you have earned your soldier; and you needn't come any more." And they went on to tell us the difficulties they had to contend with; so many being absent and would not report to them, and asked me to please let them know every now and then how the captain was getting on, and "if you need medical assistance, we will gladly respond." I thanked them heartily, and bowed myself out, and went home feeling greatly relieved. I nursed him faithfully for nearly three months, and then he was able to rejoin his command.

One morning a box was sent me from Col. Samuel D. Morgan, by a trusty friend, containing twelve thousand dollars in gold, and he said I must take care of it for him; for he was afraid it might be stolen, and added that both his family and ours might need it before the war was over. After keeping it for awhile I felt very uneasy about having such a large sum in my possession, so decided to send it back. I was so uneasy I couldn't sleep for fear some one would rob us. It was returned to Madison, Ga. In a little while it came back to me, and he said I must keep it, for he felt it was more secure in my hands. I was in a sad dilemma, not knowing what to do. I now had his $12,000 and $7,000 of our own in gold, besides watches and gold trinkets the boys had left with me for safe-keeping. I would lie awake at night and try to devise some means of safety – some secure place to hide it – and the more I thought the more I was troubled; for the servants were sharp, keen set. I worried daily, and finally took my friend, Mrs. Edgar, in whose house we lived, into my confidence, and we decided to bury it in the cellar. I got her to send her servants on errands a long distance from the house, and I told mine to take my children to walk. Then we had to hurry. I took part of the gold and ran to the cellar and hid it behind some boards and ran back for the rest. When I got in the cellar I locked the door inside. It was a long room running the length of the house, and had been used for years for sawing and stacking wood and for coal; but after locking myself in I found to my consternation that I had forgotten to bring the mattock for digging the hole to deposit it in. I wondered what I would do. I was afraid to go out for fear some one would see me and thereby excite suspicion. The only light I had was from windows with iron bars let in, so it was close and I became so excited and warm; for I imagined every minute some one would come and get in the door. I looked around and saw hanging on the wall an old rusty sword, so as quickly as I could I climbed up on a stack of wood and got it down, and on examination found I could dig with it, and my next thought was where the hole should be. I had selected a place before bringing the gold, but was afraid the keen-eyed servant boy might see fresh clay dug up and suspect something, so I decided that would not do. There was a long road in the center where the boy at different times had sawed wood, and I noticed that where the wood-horse stood there was a large pile of sawdust. I moved it out of the way and commenced to dig my hole.

It was some time before I got to the hard clay, and when I did reach it I thought I would never get out enough dirt to make the hole deep enough. But I worked and perspired, got out of breath, but was afraid to stop to rest, for there was no time to lose. I would dig awhile, then grabble the clay out with my hands, and by sheer perseverance I finally got it sufficiently deep to hold the gold. I groaned in agony over my blistered hands. Every few minutes would glance at the door and windows to see if any one was near, and I believe that if I had seen eyes peering through the windows I would have dropped on the floor from sheer excitement. But the gold was put in, and then I threw the clay on top, and with the help of a maul, which I found near by, I soon had the dirt mauled and packed in tight until it was as firm as the ground. What remaining pieces of clay I saw I gathered up in my skirt, threw it carefully behind the wood, piled the saw-dust up and mauled that, and then got some loose dust and scattered it over so it looked as if nothing had disturbed it; then put the wood-horse back just over the gold. I made my exit as soon as possible, and secretly watched to see if the boy who sawed the wood noticed anything amiss in his workshop, but he went along as usual with his duties, piling up the sawdust over the buried treasure. When the war closed, it was returned to Col. Samuel D. Morgan. I would hesitate to go through the same ordeal again, as I almost suffocated.

The siege of Vicksburg.

CHAPTER SEVENTEEN

☆ ☆ ☆ ☆

The fighting continued daily, and we would hear heartrending descriptions of the sufferings of our brave boys, fathers, and husbands. The slaughter was terrible, and often the enemy's forces numbered three or four to our one. Look at them at the siege of Vicksburg, in the trenches, for weeks holding the gunboats at bay! Look at them at Port Hudson and all down the Mississippi, having chills and fever until they looked like hickory leaves and were almost reduced to skeletons! Chills would seize them, followed by burning fevers, and they would take quinine without measuring it, and as soon as the fever would pass off, to use their expression, "they would get up and go for the Yankees again." Look at Shiloh, Gettysburg, Chickamauga, Franklin, and our brave army in Virginia, in all the numerous battles – indeed in fights everywhere! Whole regiments would form a solid line, and would be mowed down; and in a second almost a solid front would be presented again to share the same fate; and often there would hardly be left enough to form a corporal's guard.

We would hear from every division in the South of deeds of daring and bravery that could not be surpassed, and this accomplished by men with short rations and poorly clad. Talk about Washington at Valley Forge? Their sufferings could not surpass that borne by our brave boys, half clad and often barefooted because shoes could not be procured, many times their feet so swollen from weary marches and hard leather that they would have to wrap them in rags, often leaving traces of blood on the snows of Western Virginia; but in the midst of these distresses pressing on to meet the enemy. Talk about the Spartans at Thermopylæ – the charge of the brave six hundred? We had our Greeks and brave Scotch Highlanders, or their equals, in our dear Confederacy. I often thought, when our generals had to contend with such overwhelming numbers, that they might have exclaimed in anguish of spirit, as Wellington did at Waterloo: "O for night or Blucher!" But the Federals had the world to draw on for their Bluchers, but we the lifeblood of our little Confederacy. And in thinking of the difference in numbers, you will pardon me if I digress for a few minutes and mention a little fact that struck me so forcibly lately and will carry out my statement in regard to their overwhelming forces. From the pension list, thirty years after the war, we find they are paying more persons than we had soldiers in the field. I saw the list of enlisted men given a short time since, and it was over two millions, and we had six hundred thousand valiant troops from our beloved South, our husbands, sons, and brothers fighting for home and dear ones. The Government is paying Federal pensions to the uttermost parts of the earth almost – Australia, New Zealand, and every country in Europe – for their army was made up of recruits from everywhere. Any one who would fight for money was sent against us. I have done our soldiers great injustice, for instead of contending with three to one, they had six and eight to one of ours. Was such a thing ever heard of in the world's history? and just to think it lasted four long years with all our privations and sufferings, and then not whipped, but had to succumb to brute force. I think the United States ought to feel proud of the soldiers of the South, and be willing to accord them the place of honor in history they so richly deserve. We can challenge the world, and say: "Show us their equals in honor, integrity, bravery, and gallantry shown our women under all circumstances."

Faithful Old Joe

CHAPTER EIGHTEEN

☆　☆　☆　☆

Servants were hard to get, but we succeeded in finding a faithful, good woman, a negro from Virginia, who cooked for us, and with our faithful servant, Joe, who was invaluable, we got on very comfortably. Joe was the quickest, smartest negro I ever saw – always ready and willing for any emergency. I had to send him to Augusta almost every day, and I was very uneasy, so afraid he would be forced to work on the fortifications or to move cotton, for they were stacking it in the streets preparing to burn it if the enemy came. They had tried to get him several times, but he had eluded them by some cunning device. It was difficult to get hands to work, for they would hide in the day, but at night the churches would be crowded. They had a revival of religion started when we first got to Augusta, and it lasted for months. One night the officers heard of this meeting, and made a raid on the male portion, and got a good many hands for their work, but Joe jumped out of the window and made his escape. The next morning he laughed and told me about it, and said he was too smart: they couldn't "ketch" him.

One day I had occasion to send him to Augusta for something that was greatly needed, and I noticed him before starting working at his arm. He had bandaged it up tightly, and was preparing to put it in a sling. I asked him what he was doing. He said: "Miss July, my arm is broken, and you know I can't work." I was greatly amused, and for a week after that, whenever he had to go to the city, these same preparations had to be made. He always started off with a stick, and when an officer came in view he hobbled along, leaning on his stick, arm and leg both disabled. But one day they got him. He was a fine singer and celebrated jig dancer, and cut the pigeon wing to perfection, and his great desire to show off to his colored friends was the means of his capture. He saw a platform in the street, and with his crippled leg and bandaged arm mounted it and commenced a lively jig, singing in a loud voice, "Carve dat 'possum to de heart;" and just as he finished and was about to descend with great difficulty the officer laid hold of him and said: "I have been watching you for several days, and you are a slick rascal, but I have got you now and will put you to work." He tried to beg off, and told them all his white folks were sick and he was their only dependence, and he had just come in for the doctor. But all his pleading was without avail; they would listen to no excuse, and put him to work to pile cotton, and gave him some hands to help him. They had to straighten some cotton that was bulging out of line and stack it. So he went to work very cheerfully, proved a good worker, went all down the line and adjusted it, and when this was finished, he found a long row of wagons, and he had to examine them (a self-imposed task). He would crawl under and out again until he got out of sight of the cotton, and then he fairly flew home, but it was late when he got there. He laughed immoderately when he told us how he had got ahead of them again, and

I said he would have many sins to answer for in the stories he had told, but thought if he would not make himself so conspicuous he would fare better. I had to keep him at home for some time, afraid to send him to town, and it was a great deprivation to me, and particularly so to him, as he was missing so much fun and I his valuable services, but he bore his imprisonment very cheerfully.

Capt. Charlie Ewing, of Nashville, and several other boys just from the front, came to see me at this time and told me there was a great revival of religion in the army, and that Dr. John B. McFerrin, Bishop Quintard, and many other preachers of all denominations were taking part in the meetings; that the bishop had confirmed a number of the boys, and many of them were greatly concerned about their soul's salvation. They said Dr. D. C. Kelley, then Col. Kelley, had regular prayer meetings, and that Gen. Forrest attended them. Col. Kelley was on Gen. Forrest's staff, and he had great influence over the general, and when he got in a towering rage Col. Kelley could by talking to him soothe and quiet him in a few minutes. He had confidence in his colonel, for he had seen him tried many times and knew him to be fearless and brave, and he had great admiration for a brave man. I was delighted to hear such good news, for when the sun would rise in the morning we could not tell ere the day closed how many mothers' darlings would be giving up their lives for the land they loved so well.

Gen. Nathan Bedford Forrest

CHAPTER NINETEEN

☆ ☆ ☆ ☆

My *protégé*, Johnnie Bright, and my little son were greatly annoyed because they did not have new clothes, and I had resorted to patching to make them presentable. Two nephews of the lady whose house we rented had just returned from school, and had plenty of military clothes, consisting of nice jackets and an innumerable number of white linen pants, and my boys felt they were sadly neglected, and I fear they looked with envious eyes on the cadets' fine clothes. I had some of the Confederate gray left, and I told Johnnie I would have him a suit made, and he was delighted with the idea. I gave him the cloth and told him to go to Augusta to a certain tailor, have it cut, and get him to furnish the trimmings and make it. I had bought him a hat and shoes, and he only needed the suit to make his wardrobe complete. He went off in a glee, for clothing was hard to get then at any price. Every day for a week he would go in to see how the suit, or rather the making of it, was progressing. On Saturday he came home all decked in his finery, and O such a sight it was! He had made a full colonel's uniform, with a general's cap and gilt braid, stars and tassels, and to sum it all up, I never saw as much tinsel on one uniform in my life. And this was the secret of so many trips to town, giving directions about the trimmings, as I afterward learned. When I saw him, I was so convulsed with laughter I could hardly speak for some time; and when all joined in the laugh, he stood considerably abashed at his reception. It was some minutes before I could speak to so grand a gentleman, but ventured at last to ask him what his outfit cost. I had given him a large bill to have changed to pay the tailor, and he handed me a few "shinplasters," all he had left. He said a piece of the goods was left, and he thought it a pity to have any of it wasted, so he just had the cap made. His conscience began to hurt him some, for he had the new hat I had just bought him, and he thought an apology necessary. I ventured to ask so august a personage what his cap had cost, and he said he got it cheap, as trimmings were so high: he got it made for $50. Our currency had depreciated greatly by this time, and everything was scarce and hard to get.

Johnnie was not quite fifteen, had grown up like a weed, was tall and handsome and we thought he looked elegant in his suit, although he had not earned his stars and bars. He was now more determined than ever to go to the army, and he worried us so much we finally gave a reluctant consent. We got him some pins, needles, and thread, packed his clothes, fixed him a nice lunch, and he bade us an affectionate farewell. He went to town, walked around a few hours, and began to get a little homesick; so he came back, he said, to spend one more night with the children, and he would certainly start in the morning. The children were delighted at his return, as they were greatly attached to him. I told him to tell his father that we were all opposed to his going, and he said:

"Aunt Julia, you rest easy: I will make it all-right with pa."
The next morning he really started, and a few days afterward I got a letter from him saying: "A soldier offered me
five hundred dollars for my suit, but I wouldn't take a
thousand for it." The letter was filled with Latin, with the
translation above the lines. That was for the benefit of the
children, for he loved to be thought an oracle by them. In
his wanderings he had gotten a little smattering of Latin,
and he used it on all occasions. Dear Johnnie, we all loved
him, and we will never see his like again. We all missed
him after he left, and had many a merry laugh at his ex-
pense. He went through the war, and died soon after. I
never saw him again, but even now I often think of the
generous, handsome, merry, rollicking boy.

Every few days some friendly face from the army
would slip out to see us for a day and night. Often they
were sent to the rear on important business. One morning
we heard there were sixty or seventy soldiers (some
Tennesseeans) in jail, and were to be shot for desertion;
for it was deemed necessary by the officials to make ex-
amples of some of them to prevent utter demoralization
to the whole army. I learned that Albert Gentry, son of
Hon. Meredith P. Gentry, was among the number. Col.
Gentry was then at Richmond, was a member of Congress, and was considered a great orator. I had heard from
Albert's sister that he had been left at home on a farm in
Tennessee, and that he had slipped off without their
knowledge and had joined the army. He was only sixteen
years old, but well grown. His father and sister were
friends of ours, and we were greatly distressed at hearing
of the trouble the boy was in, and I determined to do all
in my power to save him from so sad a fate. I decided to
go in immediately and see what could be done, for ladies

could do more than men in cases like this. They were like the importunate widow: would persevere and take no denial. I went to see the officer who granted permits for persons to visit the jail, but he persistently refused to let any one see them. I returned home very sad and dispirited. My husband wrote to Col. Samuel D. Morgan and Judge William P. Chilton and asked them to do what they could for him. Col. Morgan wrote to President Davis to ask his help. I went again to Augusta and begged to be permitted to see my friend's son, but with no better success. I was almost in despair.

There was a Gen. Roberson from Texas whom I had met in Marietta. He had been very kind to Sister Lucy Burt when the Federals bombarded their house, and had rendered them valuable assistance in their flight. He was afterward badly wounded – had three ribs broken by a cannon ball – and I had been visiting him and taking him delicacies. The thought occurred to me that maybe he might have some influence, so I went to him and he gave me some encouragement, and told me to call again the next day, and in the meantime he would see what could be done, and said he would gladly do all in his power to help me. I went home with a lighter heart. On applying to him the next day, I found he had secured the permit, and after thanking him for his kindness and promptness, I hurried to the jail. I presented my paper with a good deal of trepidation – for I had worried so much over the case I confess I was somewhat nervous – but to my surprise, I was promptly admitted. I called for Albert Gentry. The guard said he would be down in a few minutes, and in the meantime I took a survey of his abode. I looked up and saw a good many heads and eyes peering through the grated bars at me, and such a noise above. They had a fiddle, and were playing, singing, dancing, and such stamping of feet I never heard. I thought, "Poor, young, thoughtless creatures, dancing on the brink of eternity," and I felt sick at heart; but in a little while the noise ceased, for they soon found out a lady was there.

In a short time Albert came in, and I told him who I was. I had never seen him before, but let him know that I was a friend of his father and sister, and I was greatly distressed at his situation. He asked me many questions, and I told him that from a recent letter I had heard that his father was sick and had left Richmond for some other point in Virginia, and his sister had gone home thinking he was there. He told me that he had heard nothing from them in a long time, and had got tired and slipped out and joined the army. I asked him what he was put in jail for, and he commenced sobbing, and said for desertion, but he did not intend to desert. He joined the army to fight, but wanted to do so for Tennessee, and did not want to be sent to South Carolina. He, boy-like, wanted to defend his own State, and he heard Forrest's cavalry were going to Tennessee, so he left his own command and went to Gen. Forrest, and they arrested him. I asked him if he knew that they were sentenced to be shot in three or four weeks, for a good many others were in jail for the same thing. He said he had heard their fate. After telling him I was trying to do all I could for him, I arose to leave. He begged me to come to see him again, and thanked me for my efforts and seemed to appreciate them. All the time I was talking, anxious eyes were peeping at me through the small windows. I asked Albert if I could do anything for him, and he said: "Yes, ma'am; please bring me something to eat." The other prisoners heard the request, and they yelled out: "Bring us some too; and some tobacco."

I told them that I would remember them; and such shuffling and pushing each other aside to see me, and impress on me to be sure to bring them something!

Poor boys, how sorry I felt for them, such merry, rollicking fellows under such circumstances! I stopped in Augusta and told some gentlemen friends about the tobacco, and they promised to have it ready in the morning. I hurried home, started to cooking, and prepared a large basket of as many nice things as I could collect. I took Joe and started off early the next morning with my basket loaded with supplies for the unfortunates, and got the tobacco on my way to the jail. When I got there, I called for Albert, and told him to take the basket and tobacco and go up and distribute the things among the boys. I waited until he came back, and he said that they sent many thanks to me for my kindness; that it was the best eating they had had in a long time, and they said that when I came again to please remember them. I told them I would not forget them. I went in for nearly a week, and always carried my basket well filled.

Still no news came from Richmond. The enemy was tearing up the railroads and breaking the connection everywhere. The mails were very irregular, and every two or three days Cousin Sam Morgan would write and want to know if anything had been done for the boy. In sheer desperation, I went to Gen. Roberson and told him he must help me. He said that he had worried a good deal over the case, and thought that he had found a solution to it. "At least I hope; but don't be too sanguine, for you might be disappointed. I will send a special courier to South Carolina to Gen. Johnston and state the case to him, and I think he will help us." He sent the messenger, and in a few days he came back with the good news that

Albert was released. I soon had him with us with a leave of absence for ten days, and then he was to join his command. He had been in prison long enough to be very dirty, and his clothes were in a bad condition, and he looked pitiful. I looked over and mended what few clothes he had, and supplied him with all he needed. Before his time was out he looked rested and cheerful; but I watched for the day of his return, and I had him all ready, clothes packed, a good lunch ready, and told him good-bye.

A little while after he left, his father came. He had heard of his son's trouble and came to Augusta to see about him. I never saw any one more grateful than he was for saving his son. He wept like a child when we told him what we had to contend with to get him released. He said that he thought his boy was at home on the farm, never having heard he had joined the army.

Gen. Joseph E. Johnston

CHAPTER TWENTY

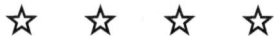

☆ ☆ ☆ ☆

We were being sorely pressed on all sides. Every man that could shoulder a musket was needed, and all in the jail were let out, I am glad to say, without a one being shot. But it gave them a good scare that lasted the rest of the war. They needed this example, for many of them were very much demoralized with the long, tedious marches, poor food, and scant clothing. They commenced to think they had the world to fight. I wonder sometimes that they persevered as long as they did without complaining.

One morning I received a message from a lady I had known in Marietta. She and her husband had been very kind to us while there. She asked me to please come over the river to Hamburg to see them. Her husband was very sick, and was so anxious to meet me. This place was in South Carolina, just across the river from Augusta. I went over, and found her husband with a hard chill. The bed he was on shook, the rigor was so great. They were in extreme poverty, having left Marietta when the enemy was near, and were not able to bring many of their things with them. The fat, jolly man had fallen off until I hardly recognized him. His face had turned from a very red to a pale color. He had been a generous eater and drinker, and the vintage had been short in South Carolina, and his purse shorter; so to sum it all up, he was in a pitiful condition. I did what I could to help them, and then said good-bye. I didn't hear anything from or about them in three or four weeks. The conscript officers were after every man that could fire a gun, and my friend's husband was among the recruits taken up. He came to Mr. Morgan in great distress, and asked him to write a note to Dr. Paul F. Eve, stating his inability to do service. He said he knew Dr. Eve was his friend, and anything he would write him would have its influence. He was very patriotic, but he didn't like the smell of gun powder. My husband told him he was not a member of the medical board, and he didn't see how he could write him a paper of disability. He had a holy horror of going into the army if there was any way to prevent it, and had his heart set on the note, and said: "Write anything you think will help me, and I believe Dr. Eve will release me." Mr. Morgan still declined, not knowing what to state; but he would take no denial. So the note was written to this effect: "Dr. Eve: Having known this gentleman and family intimately for eighteen months while in Marietta, I think that I can safely say that I do not think he is good for anything in the world." He read it over, and said: "O my friend, I will never forget you while I live. I thank you most heartily." I think that he was the first man I ever knew who thanked another for calling him a fool. Dr. Eve was a man of keen perceptions, and saw the joke and enjoyed it immensely. He gave him a letter of disability, and as long as the doctor lived he laughed over this funny incident.

CHAPTER TWENTY-ONE

☆ ☆ ☆ ☆

There were crowds of sick and wounded soldiers in Augusta, and going up Green and Broad Streets any pleasant day you would see the sidewalks thronged with them, getting the fresh air and enjoying the sunshine, many looking pale and haggard, but cheerful and bright, and if there was any fun to be had, they were always ready to enjoy it.

There was a noted belle, of Augusta, that could be seen frequently on the streets. She had a magnificent form and graceful carriage, and as she came with her stately walk she always attracted attention. A friend told me that he was standing on the pavement one day as she passed, and he noticed a pale, cadaverous, ragged soldier looking eagerly at her, and saw a merry twinkle in his eye. The lady had on a dress with a very long train to it, and as she turned the corner she looked back, and gave her skirt a slight pull. The soldier, still looking intently at her or the train, now said: "Go on, marm, it's a comin'. It's jest turnin' the corner." She blushed and hurried on.

Of course there was a hearty laugh, in which my friend joined. He said it was ludicrous in the extreme. They were so full of fun that an occasion like that was irresistible.

Old Cousin Samuel Morgan was restless with nothing to do but watch and await coming events; and as he was quite an artist, he conceived the idea of carving some pipes and pipestems as souvenirs for his children, grandchildren, and friends, to while away idle moments. There was a quantity of soft, white stone near where he lived, and he got this and carved beautiful designs and polished them highly, and they were very artistic. He made pipes of this stone and carved fishes on them that were perfectly executed, and many pipestems that had various devices on them. One had a likeness of my husband, with rod in hand, pulling out a five-pound trout. There was the man, rod, line, and fish, and you could almost imagine the sheen on the scales of the fish. They were highly prized not only as works of art, but for his sake. I mention and describe so minutely for a purpose that I will tell later on.

Our lines were drawing in closer in every direction. I was kept so busy with family affairs and soldiers coming and going that I didn't get to the hospital as often as I had formerly done. It was a great deprivation, for in going I often found many that I knew. Letters were written by me, as on former occasions, to loved ones at home bearing messages from dying boys to their mothers and sisters. I have letters now in response to some of these, full of anguish and sorrow; but such were the cruel issues of the war.

The women of the South were as brave as the men, and there was no menial office that they would not perform if it was to alleviate suffering. My husband was still at home with the Minie ball in his side, and at times suffered agony with it. He consulted several surgeons in regard to his joining his command, and they told him that

if he rode horseback he would run the risk of being para-
lyzed.

The enemy was advancing rapidly, and everything
was at fever heat. News came that Gen. Sherman was
coming, like the Duke de Alva in the Netherlands, with
torch and sword, burning as he came, for he was having
a triumphant march, gaining great victories over helpless
women and children, for our forces were scattered in every direction. Gen. Hood in Tennessee, Gen. Joe
Johnston in the Carolinas, Gen. Lee's army in Virginia,
and our cavalry trying to fight the enemy everywhere.
The Federals had such overwhelming forces that our fatigued and broken-down soldiers could not defend all the
weak points, and they were contending for every foot of
ground, and whenever they could make a stand they
would fight. Sherman advanced to attack Augusta, and
every man that could shoulder a musket was urged to
help defend the place. Mr. Morgan was restless, and he
said at last that he would take the chances and go. Col.
Stoner, of John H. Morgan's command, got him a good
horse, and Drs. Joe and Charlie Tidings, surgeons of the
same command, promised me that if he was killed or
wounded they would look after him especially. Joe
brought "Dixie" out, and after telling us good-bye, he
mounted, and in a few minutes was lost to our view. That
was as dark a day as I spent during the war. Hope seemed
all gone for a few hours, for when I thought of the sacrifices made by our people, and the privations they endured, I wondered how they could be unrewarded. The
soldiers still hoped that something would happen to turn
the tide of battle in our favor. They were the last ones to
give up, and "Onward!" was their cry.

There was severe fighting going on fifteen or

twenty miles from Augusta, in South Carolina. The next bulletin announced that Gen. Sherman had burned Columbia, S.C., and that many persons had perished in the flames. And news followed this speedily that the Federals were in sight of Augusta, and that they were burning everything in their reach. You could hear anything and everything that was horrible. Alas! much that we heard was too true, and we looked upon Gen. Sherman as a monster in human shape, and now that the grave has closed over him he will have a big account to settle for his treatment of the South in her last struggles.

The next morning after my husband left, some one came in and told me that they saw my little son running in the direction of Augusta with his gun on his shoulder. He said that he was going in the trenches to help defend Augusta. Fortifications were being thrown up, and every preparation was being made to save the place, and every man and boy was eager to help. There was a crowd going in to report for duty. I called Joe and told him to run as fast as his feet could carry him, and bring my little son back before he was lost in the mass of men. I was so excited I walked the yard, straining my eyes in the direction of the city. He was gone two hours, and it seemed an interminable time before I saw Joe coming with him. He said that he had hunted a long time, and finally saw him, and had to force him to come, by telling him that he would take him in his arms and carry him whether or not. This would have been a terrible insult to a soldier, so he followed Joe home very reluctantly. I took his gun and told him not to touch it again without my consent, and if he did I would break it all to pieces, for he might have had his head blown off and no one would have known whose child he was in that great crowd. He saw from the mood

I was in that I was prepared to do what he would have thought the greatest calamity of his life, for he prized his gun more than anything he possessed. My threat had the desired effect, for he stayed at home closely after this.

I had heard no news from Mr. Morgan, and I felt restless and miserable all the time. There was rumor of a fight, and many were supposed killed and wounded, but we had no way of learning the real truth. One night about 10 o'clock I heard the rattle of wheels, and then a vehicle stopped at my front door. I took a light and ran out and saw Drs. Joe and Charlie Tidings. I said: "Where is Mr. Morgan?" They replied: "In the ambulance." They told me not to be alarmed, he was hurt, but they hoped not seriously, and then lifted him out carefully and brought him in the house. They then told me that twenty miles from Augusta they had met a large force of Gen. Sherman's cavalry, and as they were making a double-quick charge Mr. Morgan's horse got his leg in a sand hole. The horse fell on him and nearly killed him, and but for the prompt assistance of his friends, who jumped down and lifted the horse off, he would have been dead in a little while. They got him to the rear as soon as possible. He had a violent contusion of the hip, and was badly bruised all over; but if he had no internal injuries, they thought that he would pull through all right. They remarked: "It is God's providence that he wasn't killed, for where he fell eighty were killed and wounded." They remained all night, examined him in the morning, and gave me explicit directions what to do for him, and bade us good-bye. That was the last that I ever saw of those two good men, but I will always feel grateful to them for their kindness to me and mine during the war. Mr. Morgan was confined to his bed for some time, and when he did get up he had to use crutches for many months.

Not many days after this we got a letter from Col. Sam Morgan, saying that the enemy was near Blackwell, S.C. He was living there with his daughter, having gone there when Sherman took Marietta. He said that he would send all of his family to our house, and for me to do the best that I could with them. I went to the car at the stated time of arrival with my carriage at their service, but after consultation with his daughter, found that room could not be made for all, for my family was large and so was theirs, and our rooms were limited. So they decided that it was best to remain in the car until further arrangements could be made. I took his four granddaughters out with me, and left the others in the car. They soon decided to go up to Madison, Ga. I kept the four girls for awhile, and two days after two nieces of my husband ran over from Montgomery to spend a few days, not dreaming of the disasters that were so soon to come upon us. I had now my old kinsman's four granddaughters, four nieces (two of them lived with us), and my two daughters – ten girls – and a merrier, jollier crowd never got together. They did not brood over troubles like the old people, and I was glad to see them so happy. Now how they were to sleep was the next question, and they told me to leave it all to them and they would arrange it.

The Montgomery girls left in a short time, fearing they might be cut off from their home. The girls told me that they were compelled to have some clothes laundered. I sent all around to hire a washerwoman, as my servant was sick, and I was afraid for her to undertake it; but no negro could be got for love or money, as they were all too much excited looking for the Yankees. The girls were in a sad dilemma, and none of them had ever tried the washtub. They had a long consultation, and came to the conclusion that if Joe would bring the water and set the kettle to boiling, they would roll up their sleeves and play the Biddies. So Joe very promptly had the pot boiling, adjusted the tubs and washboards, and such scrubbing, laughing, and chattering you have not heard in some time. They made a regular frolic of it, and every now and then they would call on Joe for more water or some other service. He danced attendance on them through it all. It was a ludicrous sight. I have laughed over it many times. They finally got through the first and last washing they ever did in their lives, and they all joined in and soon had the clothes ironed. All pronounced it a success, but it left blisters on their hands. I may not get the dates of certain events just at the right time, for in thirty years I have forgotten many things that transpired. In a short time the girls went to Madison, to their grandfather, and mine returned to Eatonton to school.

One morning the news came that Gen. Lee had surrendered, and the next day it was confirmed. We both wept like children. The next news was that Gen. Sherman had taken Augusta, and he had sent a detachment of soldiers to the Sand Hills to take possession of the arsenal near us. In the course of the day I heard a noise, and on looking out, saw sure enough a long line of blue coats, drums beating, banners waving, negroes running, shouting, yelling, looking like lunatics just escaped from the asylum. Among the number, my cook ran by me, with her white apron tied to the end of a broomstick, shouting and cheering at the highest pitch of her voice, jumped the fence, and was gone. Joe walked out into the yard with the children, and said: "I am so mad with them fool niggers. If they are free, they are free, but not to make fools of themselves." He said: "Now, if you please, look at the poor, white trash them niggers is running after. If they was in the gutters they wouldn't pick them up, unless they wanted them to fight for them. I tell you now they won't get dis nigger. And I thank God I know who my friends are." I agreed with him, that he had some sense and reason, and the other poor, silly creatures did not know what they were doing. I told him that he was my only dependence, and he must stay and cook supper for us. He readily consented, and went to work as if nothing had happened.

After dark, Celia, my cook, came back, utterly exhausted and said that she was tired almost to death, but still she went to work to pack up her clothes. I went to her room and asked her what she intended to do. She said: "I am packing up all my things, for I am going to start to Virginny to-morrow, to see my children." I told her that I did not blame her for wanting to find her children, but if she started she would have to walk most of the way, as the railroads were torn up in every direction. I liked the negro, she had been faithful and trustworthy, and I told her that if she would wait until I went to Nashville I would pay her way to Richmond.

She looked undecided and I said: "Don't you believe me? Did I ever tell you anything but the truth?"

She said: "No, ma'am, but, missus, is I free?"

I told her yes, to put her clothes away and behave herself. I did not want to see her start and maybe die in a fence corner by herself. She seemed perfectly satisfied. But in a few days was taken quite sick from the effects of the tramp after her deliverers. She grew worse, and I sent to Augusta for Dr. Joseph Eve, and he pronounced her very ill. She had been a delicate negro before this, and the present excitement added fuel to the fire, and in a few days after, we found that she would not recover. By the time I got through with doctors' bills and funeral expenses, I found I had paid out many dollars in gold for the poor, simple creature.

I now had to depend on Joe for everything – we made him both maid and waiting boy, and he proved competent and willing, for faithfully he performed his part.

The next morning the children came running in, and, said: "Papa, papa! A whole lot of Yankees are coming up the front walk." And they all began crying and begging him not to go out, for they thought his time had come to be captured. He told them that he would go out to meet them, for he could not help himself. So he started, followed by the children and myself. He walked clown a short distance in advance, and I heard him say: "Why, howdy, boys? We thought you were Yankees coming to arrest me."

The party consisted of Gen. Basil Duke, Dr. Robert Williams, a son-in-law of cousin Sam Morgan, Charlton, Richard, Calvin, and Key Morgan. These were all the Lexington Morgans left, as John H. Morgan and Thomas, his brother, had been killed some time before this. There was quite a large party of them, including servants.

The latter had on blue clothes, and the children had mistaken them for Federals. They said: "We have just left President Davis. We cut across the country and made for your house, and we want to stay here until we can send to Augusta and see what Gen. Sherman's terms of surrender will be. If favorable, we will have to take the oath and go home; if not, we will get on our horses, and try to cross the Mississippi River, then into Texas and Mexico." After consultation it was agreed that Dr. Williams should go in to see the Federal authorities.

In the meantime I was running back and forth trying to find them something to eat. The servants fed the horses, and then I pressed them into service, and with Joe to help, we soon had dinner ready for them. I had strong coffee and tea made, and when it was all ready they sat down and did full justice to it. Then the pipes were called for. We had enough tobacco, but not enough pipes and stems to go around, so we called Joe, and submitted the case to him, and he said that in a little while he could fix some cob pipes. He had some stems. He came back in a short time with those he had made, but still they lacked some; so Mr. Morgan called on me for my beautifully carved stems and pipes. I gave them up rather reluctantly, as I had set my heart on keeping them as specimens of art, but I soon gladdened the hearts of those who were anxious to smoke. They were all restless, and all were looking eagerly for Dr. Williams's return, but he did not get back till late in the afternoon, and brought the good news that the terms were honorable. In a short time their horses were saddled, and I brought out their treasures I had in safekeeping for them for some time. They consisted of watches and other gold trinkets, and bars of silver they had gotten in Richmond when paid off as soldiers. They went to Augusta, took the oath, and then started for their homes.

I have the stems and pipes with the nicotine in them from the smoking they did that memorable day of agony, and they have never been used since.

By this time the Federals were all over the country, and we learned that when Marietta was burned, our home there was untouched, as the general in command took it for headquarters, and had a flag stretched across the front of the house, and I suppose that saved it. We did not care to stop in Marietta. Our hearts were yearning for home and loved ones, and "Onward to Nashville!" was the cry.

Mr. Morgan went in advance of us to see what arrangements he could make for taking us home and in a little while he wrote to my nephew to bring us on. We soon had everything in readiness, and bade our Georgia friends farewell with sad hearts, for they had greatly endeared themselves to us by their kindness during our sojourn with them.

We started, going by Madison, where we were joined by Cousin Sam Morgan and family, also our girls, who had come over from Eatonton to meet us on our way to Nashville, and among others who composed the party were John H. Morgan's widow and little daughter and Miss Alice Ready. While passing up the road we saw signs of Gen. Sherman's work; he did it well and thoroughly. It had been raining a great deal, and on the clay hills were many tents filled with women and children, with mud and slush all around, and heaps of ashes, and smokeless chimneys standing as lone sentinels in the devastated and waste places. Many Confederate soldiers were wending their way home on foot to take up the thread of life. They were ragged, tired, weary, and sorefooted, with the glint still in their eyes. In looking at them, I thought of a little verse I had seen in early life.

> I see a man: I do not see his shabby dress,
> I see him in his manliness,
> I see his ax, I see his spade,
> I see a man that God has made.
> If such a man before you stand,
> Give him your heart, give him your hand,

And praise your Maker for such men.
They make this old world young again.

I felt like giving each one my hand and bidding
them "Godspeed." All needed the ax and spade when
they did get home to build up demolished houses; and,
Phoenix-like, they rose from their ashes, built up their
homes, planted crops, and have given many millions to
educate white and colored, and are paying a greater part
of the pensions to Union soldiers. They are, in short, as-
tonishing the world, all going to show that the Scotch,
Irish, Huguenot, and Cavalier blood cannot be kept
down. If Gen. Sherman's idea had been carried out,
which was, as fast as we were turned out of our homes,
to bring in those from the North and colonize, we would
now have been no better than Russian serfs; but the old
man made suggestions and nursed his wrath to keep it
warm. Another one of his ideas was to give the negroes
the torch and sword and let them burn and slay as they
chose, but the enlightened nineteenth century would
never have submitted to the warfare of the Dark Ages on
this American Continent. If he had a kind word to say, or
one of encouragement to his fallen brother, no one ever
heard it. How different with heroic Gen. Grant! He had
the elements of a brave man and a heart that could feel
for the infirmities of others. Look at him at Appomattox
Courthouse when Gen. Lee surrendered! Behold the two
men! Gen. Lee stately, upright, standing in his physical
beauty, and on looking at him Gen. Grant doubtless felt
he was in the presence of his peer, "a foeman worthy of
his steel." Gen. Lee, conscious of dignity, rectitude, gallantry, chivalry, and a pure Christian character, stood and
faced his conqueror. Did Gen. Grant show any exultation

over his fallen foe? No, he was too magnanimous for that. I have been told that a casual observer could not have decided who was the victor or the vanquished from their faces, as both looked sad. Gen. Grant, as he conceived in line of duty to impose such humiliation on so brave and great a man, doubtless felt sad. Gen. Lee, feeling he had struggled with his brave army as few men ever did, by having to contend with privations and hardships almost unheard of, overwhelming numbers, and after having done all that a man could do in fighting for just and righteous cause, to have to succumb. He felt almost crushed and broken-hearted, but did he give up the battle of life? Not he! He went to work again and died in the harness. I believe that history will give him the place of the greatest and best man that ever trod this American Continent. What did Gen. Grant do? He spoke kind words to his vanquished brother and tried to heal dissensions, and his last plea in life was for peace. We cannot but feel pleasure in contemplating such a man.

I have often tried to imagine the return of our valiant soldiers to their homes after an absence of four years. When they left them peace and plenty reigned; farms with cattle on every hilltop, and in valleys long rows of cabins filled with happy inmates, and everything to make the heart glad. But now desolation seemed to reign. Homes burned, cattle gone, forests cut down, fences torn down, and negroes freed. Nothing left but helpless wife and children, and some of the poor fellows with legs, and some with arms gone, and many almost shot to pieces; the same proud spirit with the will to work, but physically disabled. Did you ever hear one say that he was ashamed of his wounds? No. Napolean's "Legion of Honor" were never prouder of their scars than were these old veterans;

and their faces would light up when they would give the accounts of the battles where they were maimed and mutilated for life. We have heard of a very few truckling, pusillanimous spirits that have gone North, and for filthy lucre's sake have sold their manhood, and have said that they were ashamed of the part that they had taken in our struggle. All the harm that I wish them is that they will never pollute the soil of our "Sunny South" with their unhallowed feet. And I know that brave Northern soldiers can have only contempt for such craven spirits.

Ought we of the South ever to see one of her brave veterans suffer? It would be a shame and a blot on the escutcheons of our fair land to permit it. Although many years have passed, and very little has been done, everything points to the time when they will be cared for. Look at the efforts of our few noble women in securing the Confederate Home. They commenced with very little encouragement, and have plodded patiently and perseveringly until I am rejoiced to say that their untiring efforts are being crowned with success. God bless them in their holy undertaking! and may their efforts stimulate our men that fortune has smiled upon since the war, and impel them to take some of their hundreds of thousands, and even millions, and make the old veterans' hearts glad! Many of them are going down the other side of the hill, and are weary and worn, straggling with penury and want. If I had the power, I would pension every one of them, and not give it as doling out charity, but let them feel that they had earned it and had a right to it. Go on, grand women of the South, in your hallowed work, and don't give up until your end is accomplished. Our men are too chivalrous not to give aid when they see the efforts of their mothers, sisters, and wives trying to do what duty ought to impel them to perform. When your noble work has been carried through, and after "life's fitful dream is o'er," take your children and spread flowers over their graves, and never let them forget the brave heroes that sleep their last sleep in the land they loved so well as to lay down their lives defending it. So impress it on their young minds that when we go to give an account of our stewardship the story shall be repeated to the children, grandchildren, and great-grandchildren, so that "Old Mortality" shall not have to come along to scrape off the moss and mold to read the inscription on the tombstones that mark the resting place of our noble dead.

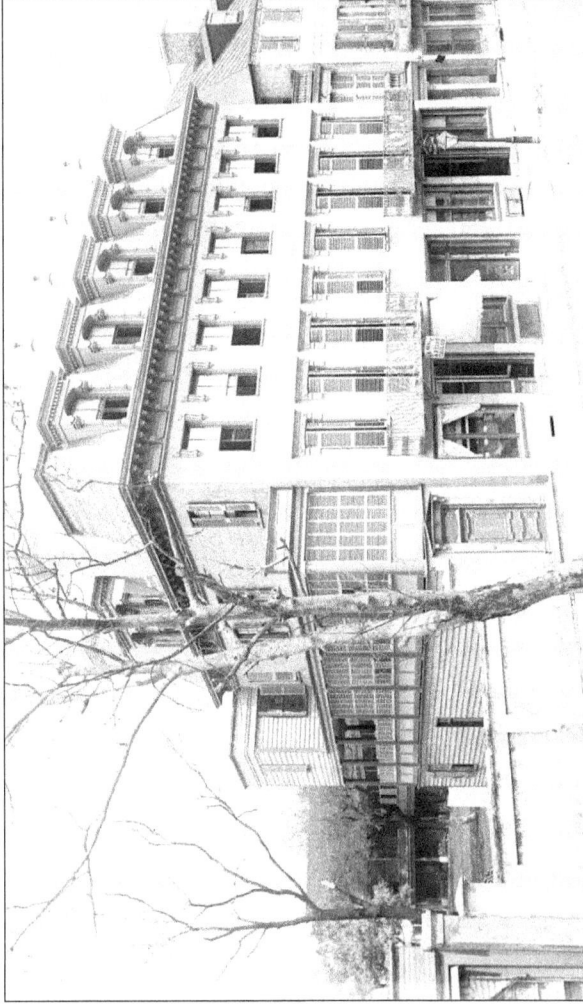

The Confederate Home in Charleston, S.C.

CHAPTER TWENTY-TWO

☆ ☆ ☆ ☆

As we passed through Marietta I looked to see the homes of friends who had shown us so many delicate attentions, and had been so good nursing our brave boys. But there, too, the work of Gen. Sherman was well done, as there was nothing left in many cases but heaps of bricks and ashes.

We got to Chattanooga, and such a desolate, dreary looking place it was, for it had been raining, and the red clay was shoe deep. It had been the center and distributing point for the Federals, and crowds of troops were still there, besides thousands who had taken up temporary abodes. My nephew was trying to get our baggage. The children were worn out and crying, but we all started to walk to the hotel, which was a short distance off. Joe headed the procession with two of the children in his arms; the rest of us, plunging along, would slip in mudholes, and such scrambling as we would have to keep from falling; and to add to the trouble, it was one of the darkest, gloomiest nights that I ever saw, and the depot and surroundings were poorly lighted. We finally reached the hotel, bedraggled and weary, and went to our rooms, were we ate our lunch from a basket that I had brought with us.

After being much refreshed from our night's rest, we started the next morning for Nashville. My baby and the next one were especially devoted to Joe, and wanted him with them all the time. He amused them continually, and I told him to stay in sight, so if I wanted anything I could call him, and he promised to do so. The cars were filled with Federal soldiers, walking up and down and watching every movement. They spied Joe standing by the children and ordered him out, and when the children saw him start, they began to yell and scream, and would not be pacified for some time. I told the soldiers that I had tried to get a maid, but did not succeed, and that Joe was almost indispensable to me, for the little ones were attached to him, and they were very tired, and I needed him to help me. Several of the Federals came and sat down near the children and began to talk to them. The train stopped for a few minutes, and the children spied some blackberries, and turned and said: "Lankees, get me some berries." And before I had hardly heard their request, two of them stepped off and got a handful. In the meantime the cunning Joe was watching an opportunity to get back, and in a little while he walked in with a bucket of water, which he politely handed to the ladies first, and then to the soldiers, and then he said something to the children and started to go out, as he found that they were watching him so closely. They screamed at him, and said: "Joe, come back and look at them Lankees." They were so intent in watching the "bluecoats" that they got all around them to laughing. Many of the passengers were refugees returning home. Many of them had left dear ones behind under the sod. They were depressed and tired with delays, so the children, Joe, and "the Lankees" helped to relieve the monotony, and Joe, by his kind attentions to all, was allowed to come back to his pets.

We finally reached Nashville, and I went to my sister's and stayed until we could get possession of our house. Then I learned of the many changes that had taken place in the four years. Many were in deep mourning for dear ones killed in the numerous battles fought. Many of the old citizens had passed away, while others had spent months in the prisons for not taking the oath, and large sums of money had been extorted from the citizens to support idle negroes and poor white people who had followed the Federals here.

I had received very few letters, and those unsatisfactory, while away, as all had to be submitted to the military authorities for inspection. I learned that the old Academy, my dear Alma Mater, had been stripped of everything, and my mind reverted to my childhood and to the eight happy years that I had spent there; to the cabinet of curiosities, containing shells from all parts of the world, and many rare specimens of art; to the immense library, and the numbers of pianos. All these accumulations of years were packed up and sent North to enrich some Yankee officers' families. The old empty house was left standing as a monument of one of the largest and most successful female schools in the South, and Dr. C. D. Elliot, as Principal, was much beloved, and was considered a prince of educators.

A friend moved into our house and kept it from being turned into a Federal hospital. We had to pay a large sum of money before we got our house released from the Freedman's Bureau, and thanks to our old servants, found most of our furniture scattered around among different friends, where they had placed it for safe-keeping before going to Washington.

After we had been home several days, a number

of the girls' friends came to see them. They were upstairs having a jolly time, all talking at once, when the doorbell rang. I went to open it, and there stood eight or ten Federal soldiers on the porch. I began to tremble, and was greatly startled, and thought: "What have I said that could have been reported to them, and maybe cause my arrest?" For from the time of my arrival I had tried to be very prudent in expressing myself, and felt all the time that I was almost in purgatory. Down south we had had full scope, and now that we were almost too full for utterance we had to bridle our tongues, and it was a great deprivation. We were advised that if we did talk, to close our doors and watch the keyholes. Well, there I was, confronting all those soldiers. I at last ventured to ask what they wanted. They were so engaged looking up at the pretty girls (for by this time every window was filled with heads, eager to see what was the matter) that they scarcely noticed me. I waved my hand to the young folks, and they immediately left, and then I got the soldiers' attention and asked them again what they would have. They all seemed in great glee, and said that they had been in the army a great while and had been paid off to go home, but hated to go back without seeing something of the ladies of the South, and they wanted me to board them for two or three weeks, and said that they would pay me well. You can imagine my disgust, in the frame of mind that I was in then, but I had to present a smiling face and tell them that it was impossible, as I had a very large family, and that all of my rooms were full; but they still insisted. I told them that there were many hotels and boarding houses, but they seemed determined to force themselves on us. While they talked I scanned them close-ly, and saw that they were dressed very conspicuously and had on a good deal of "pinch back" jewelry. They were very anxious to make an impression, and I wanted so badly to tell them my opinion of them, and I was really afraid that they would force themselves on us anyway; but they finally left, though they seemed greatly disappointed, and not in a good humor.

Almost every night murders were committed, and we on the east side were almost afraid to leave our homes after dark. On the bridge and down the avenue many were assaulted and robbed; and it behooved all the Rebels to be very quiet, as Nashville was still full of troops, and none of us felt very safe. One day we heard that Gen. Joseph Wheeler had been knocked down and badly beaten the night before for no other reason than that he had been an "accursed Rebel general."

Mr. Morgan was furious, for he was much attached to Gen. Wheeler, as were all of his command. No notice had been taken of the cowardly assault by the authorities, so we determined to try to find out the truth. After hunting nearly all the morning, we heard that he was at a house on High Street. So we went and rang the bell, and a lady answered. We asked if Gen. Wheeler was there, and she said: "Yes; in a room upstairs." We found him in bed and badly bruised and beaten. He said that he had had no warning of any danger, and that before he knew it he was on the ground, and a burly soldier pounding him, and he a small man and totally unarmed, not prepared in any way to defend himself. He told us that only a few had been to see him. To tell the whole truth, people at that time did not know what to do or how to act. We expressed great sympathy to our noble friend, stayed with him some time, and were very sorry that we were unable to give the ruffian his deserts.

Many long months passed, fraught with bitterness

and uneasiness. The people of the South felt that they were overcome but not conquered, and many a bitter pill they had to swallow, submitting to the inevitable.

The last time that I ever saw our brave hero, Gen. Forrest – a little while before his death – was at a large barbecue given by my husband. He was faint and weak then, and had to be supported on the grounds, but was anxious to meet many of his old comrades for the last time on earth. Since then many more have gone over the river, where they rest under the shade of the tree of life. The great reunion will come some day, when the long parted will meet, and the sword of the Christian warfare will be laid down, and eternal rest will be theirs.

The faithful Joe of our war experience is still with us, having been with us almost constantly during and since the war. Not long since we had his likeness taken, that each child and grandchild should have one of our faithful old friend. He often relates thrilling episodes of his experience during the rebellion, and still clings to his "white folks."

We are now old and gray-headed, and we sit by the fire and tell our children and grandchildren of the deeds of daring heroism and bravery of our dear soldiers who sleep on many a hilltop and valley. They died defending a cause that they felt to be just. I teach the children to hate war and all its horrors, and to love peace; but to always love and reverence the memory of our brave soldiers, and when all prejudices and animosities shall have been buried our heroes' stars will blazen forth in the galaxy of fame with a brightness and effulgence that may have been equaled, but never surpassed in the world's history.

LETTERS

☆ ☆ ☆ ☆

These are a few of the many letters we received during the war. They are given to show how we commenced arming our soldiers for the four years' fight. Many of our guns, made to carry Minie balls, were manufactured at our little gun factory in Nashville.

Montgomery, May 18 1862.

To Hon. L.P. Walker, Secretary of War.

Dear Sir: I am satisfied of your disposition to comply with Tennessee's request, so far as it is consistent to do so under the circumstances.

In view of the patent facts, both of the scarcity and pressure for arms, I have conceived the idea of converting all the rifles in Tennessee of sufficient weight into as nearly as possible a uniform length and uniform caliber, and adopting for their use the Minie ball. This use of the Minie ball explains all of the difference between the effectiveness of modern rifles and the Tennessee or Kentucky gun. By this scheme I am fully warranted in saying that all our deficiencies may be supplied.

What do you think of it? I am ready and willing to be devoted to its accomplishment.

Awaiting your answer I am your obedient servant,

Irby Morgan

Montgomery, May 14, 1861.

To Hon. L. P. Walker,

Dear Sir: The inclosed letters will explain the nature of my business with you. Tennessee is without arms, and has no other hope of getting them than out of the abundance represented to be in the possession of the Confederate Government. By the late act of the Tennessee Legislature it was determined to raise fifty-five thousand troops, twenty-five thousand to be at once under the control of the Confederate Government, and the balance, thirty thousand, to be held as reserve for contingencies. There is no mistake about the raising of the required number, or one hundred thousand, if necessary, but we have no arms to place in the hands of this gallant host of Rebels, and the question arises where shall the supply come from? It is in my judgment of the very highest possible importance that a wise, timely, prompt, liberal, confiding line of policy be adopted toward that people, not that they are likely to backslide from this position, which has been a source of so much rejoicing to us all, by no means, but that she may realize for herself in the hour of her need the fact that your foresight had prepared you for every event, controlled by human agency, and that you are ready and willing to fulfill your promises to her.

To have undertaken this great revolution unprepared, unadvised, and without a comprehensive view of the whole ground was to have been guilty of great folly, and it is at this particular juncture of equal importance, with reference to moral effect, that Tennessee's estimate of this great movement shall suffer no injury at your hands.

If I could possibly have an interview with you, I could give you many good reasons, not properly to be undertaken by letter. I am expected to telegraph the substance of the result of my conference with you on this subject, to headquarters, at Nashville, during to-day. Any communication you may be pleased to address me will reach me at once at the office of Messrs. Chilton & Yancey.

Awaiting your reply, I am your obedient servant,
Irby Morgan.

Nashville, May 7, 1861.

To Hon. W.P. Chilton Montgomery.

Mr. Irby Morgan, who is just starting to Louisville, Ky., on public business, requested me to enclose to you these caps as the first make of Nashville. They are making millions now of the same sort. Mr. M. bought the copper in Orleans, and other fixings, and says please attend to his request per his express to you from Orleans.

Respectfully yours,
C.D. Sanders.

Nashville, May 4, 1861.

Dear Irby: Since writing you to-day, suggesting the removal of the Harper's Ferry machinery to Nashville, it has occurred to me that if the scheme meets favor at the hands of President Davis, that in order to have it here in the quickest possible time, that if you could do so consistently, that you might tender your services, go at once to Gov. Seldon with the proper credentials, and get his consent for its removal out of reach of accident. If Richmond should be taken – and that is highly probable, or, at least, the attempt probable – the first act of the invaders would be to destroy every machine or tool with which arms could be made. If this would not be done, Lincoln would show a great want of judgment in conducting the war.

Yours,

S.D. Morgan.

———————

Nashville, May 13, 1861.

To Irby Morgan, Esq., care of Hon. W.P. Chilton, Montgomery, Ala.

Dear Sir: Since writing you yesterday, I have received by express, without any advices, an Enfield rifle, which, I presume, has been sent me by Judge Chilton. It is the most superior arm for a soldier I have ever seen. I do not think it can be improved. It is simple, strong, and light. I can have them made here just as good as the sample, and I can find all the material necessary right in our own city. Every piece of machinery necessary can be contracted for here also, as well as at any other place in the world, and, if need be, I can certainly get as many workmen from England as I want, or even from Yankeedom.

I will send you samples of our caps by express to-day.

In haste,

S.D. Morgan.

————————

Night of April 24, 1861.

To Irby Morgan.

Dear Irby: In the hurry of business, I forgot this evening to ask you to whose care I should address any communications to you whilst in New Orleans. Bear in mind, I shall address you, if need be, to the care of Perkins & Co. Perkins is full of zeal and energy, and will make you an able adjunct in your purchases, and, if need be, have your checks cashed by the banks (and which, by the way, they should do at par, as we are preparing to defend Louisiana and New Orleans more than ourselves).

I think you should see the Governor even if you have to go to Baton Rouge, for he certainly must have to spare some munitions or arms for the purpose we want them. We shall be forced, if possible, to dislodge the troops from Cairo. To do this we should have more arms and ammunition, and especially some field artillery, which, it seems to me, will not be as valuable to Louisiana as to Tennessee. Perkins can attend to forwarding by railroad anything you may purchase. See if good blankets can be had, the number, etc., and telegraph me, as we may probably have to order some. Look also for good shoes suitable for soldiers. Keep me well advised of your movements.

S.D. Morgan.

From Gen. John Hunt Morgan

To Irby Morgan.

Dear Sir: In a few days I leave for Knoxville. I shall remain a few days, previous to making another long trip. I hope the uniforms I ordered are complete.

Would like very much to have one thousand more of the same kind made at once, if possible. My men are in want of clothing, and I will be prepared to pay for what you have furnished. I have now upon my rolls 4,000 men, but how long they will let them remain with me I cannot tell. My last trip from Kentucky was quite successful. Carefully destroying all rail communication from Franklin to Nashville, every bridge and trestle being burned, which I am satisfied is the cause of the Federals not having advanced farther as yet. They are camped on and near the Cumberland. Now, from Nashville to near Carthage, my advanced regiment is encamped in a few miles of them. We are taking prisoners every day: yesterday, 160; to-day, 50. Since leaving the army, one month since, have captured 1,000 and paroled them.

I cannot understand the movements of our army, am fearful that we are going to enact the same programme as last winter, fall back all the time. This portion of Tennessee is worth all the rest of the State to us, containing all that our army requires. Half the proper exertions in getting provisions are not being made, and instead of falling back (at present) we ought to push forward, and consume and send back all the provisions and stock in this portion of the State, for the enemy are not prepared at this time to give battle, and if we would only advance twenty-five miles, they would certainly fall back; but it really seems to me that our generals are always preparing to fall back, as the enemy approaches, and will not rest until they
get a big river between them.

I have to-day applied to be permitted to take my crowd across into Kentucky, and to break up all communication between their army and Louisville, which will certainly prevent the advance of their army until the rivers rise, and can supply themselves by transports. A large army cannot be subsisted upon the country. Nearly all the cavalry should be sent into Kentucky and completely destroy all communication by rail and pike, and at the same time be relieving the South of at least ten thousand men, who are feeding upon her very vitals at present.

Love to cousin.

Yours very truly,

John H. Morgan,
Colonel Commanding Brigade.

Headquarters, Hartsville,
August 24.

To Irby Morgan.

Dear Sir: Before I left Knoxville I wrote you to have me made 500 more uniforms of same quality as the others. My command has grown so rapidly that I will have to get you to have made 500 more, being 1,000. Have them done as soon as you can. My men are nearly out of clothes. Have them made full size, and very strong. Our service is very hard upon clothes. I shall depend upon you furnishing me 1,000 uniforms, and have them made up as soon as possible. We have had a succession of brilliant affairs for the last six or eight days. You will see an account in the paper I send. The newspaper is edited and published in my command. I send my reports in printed form to Richmond. We are enjoying ourselves very much.

These people are the most loyal I ever met, and treat us like princes. The ladies are both beautiful and clever. The railroad from Franklin, to within eight miles of Nashville, is completely destroyed.

The tunnel above Gallatin we burned, and it cannot be opened in less than three months. All the frame work was burned, and the rock fell in, and is still burning. It is a slate rock containing coal. We destroyed every bridge. The Yankees have gone up the road, and are now using the other one by Springfield. It is a great blow to them. Gen. Nelson passed up the middle pike, day before yesterday, with a portion of his command, to Bowling Green.

I am satisfied they are leaving Nashville and preparing to make a stand at Bowling Green. We have been in this place some ten days. You can see how far we are in the advance of our whole army. Have had as many as five thousand Federals between us and the army since we came here, but the result has been that we have accomplished more than any division of our Western army.

We found the people out of heart and spirits; they had given up all prospects of being relieved. They are now all wide-awake and are joining the army rapidly. I am getting from fifty to sixty men per day from Kentucky, and without any assistance from Richmond. Nearly every gun, and all my equipments, we captured from the Federals. I send to-day to Knoxville Gen. Johnson and his officers, whom we captured.

Give my love to cousin, and tell her to kiss the little ones for me.

I hope to see you in Madison soon.

Yours truly,

John H. Morgan.

Colonel Commanding Brigade.

P.S. – You can let the editors of Atlanta see my proclamation.

———————

Headquarters, Lexington, Ky.,
October 6, 1862.

Dear Uncle Sam: I have just returned from a very fatiguing trip in the mountains, where I have been impeding the retreat of Gen. Morgan from Cumberland Gap, and consequently did not hear with certainty of the death of poor Sam until my arrival at this place. Allow me to mingle my grief with yours in this sad bereavement, so sudden, so severe that I can scarcely realize it. You have this consolation: that your gallant son died in the discharge of his duty, with his face to the foe. His last words were: "Tell my father that I died for my country."

Sam, as you well know, entered my command as a private. His unassuming bravery and strict attention to his duty soon elevated him to rank of lieutenant, and soon after to that of captain. His impartial justice and attention to the wants of his men rendered him very much beloved, and deeply do they mourn his loss. How sad that a career which opened so brightly should have been so suddenly checked by the base treachery of a foe who fired after the token of surrender was given.

Basil Duke informed me that he has already written to you, giving you the particulars of his death, and I will not therefore recount them. I write simply to testify my love and appreciation of Sam's worth, and to assure you that long will his memory be cherished with affection.

Your sincere friend,
John H. Morgan.

———————

Knoxville, Tenn., June 24 1862.

Dear Irby: I wrote you the other day from Chattanooga in reference to purchasing cloth for my men, and before I left there – through mistake, I suppose – the cloth came to my address. I sent it back to you, as I desire to have you attend to having it made up. Please have it worked up by the measure sent as rapidly as possible, and also let me know when I shall send money, and how much. Remember me very kindly to Cousin Julia and your very interesting little girls and boys.

Yours truly,
J. H. Morgan.

———————

To Mr. I. Morgan.

Dear Sir: I send you by express $5,500, which you will take care of for me, if you please. It is too much trouble to carry about, and any expenditures you make for my command can be taken from it. As soon as the uniforms are complete, please send them up with account of all expenses, and I will then give orders for any others I may require. Give my love to cousin and the children.

Very truly yours,
J. H. Morgan,
Colonel.

P. S. – Paper very scarce. We will start for Kentucky in a few days, and we will be heard from.

Johnnie's Letter on His Way to Join the Army

Griffin, Ga.,
August 18 1864.

To Mrs. Irby Morgan, Augusta, Ga.

Dear Aunt Julia: I arrived at this place Sunday at 1 o'clock, in which I found Pa and Collins doing well. Collins is improving very fast. His wound has been very severe. The gangrene ate a tremendous hole in his leg, but I think it has been killed out. I think it will take three or four months before he can walk on his leg. Mr. Southgate, of Nashville, died; John Shooks, of Fayetteville, died; Major Miller's leg was taken off. There are two hundred wounded in Griffin now. There are a great many of the Lincoln County boys here. One just from there told me Hal McKinney has taken the oath. I never once thought that it was Hal. Willie McEwin came out. We had five brigades of cavalry in Sherman's rear, between Dalton and Chattanooga. They passed though Marietta and burned part of it. A great many commissary stores also were burned. On my travel I saw a great many Yankees that our men had captured. One of them came up to me and asked me for something to eat. He told me that if I would give him something to eat he would give me a housewife. I told him that I wanted to see him starve awhile first. When I reached Macon, he asked me again, and I gave him a piece of corn bread; then he gave me the housewife. It was the prettiest I ever saw. He said that he hated to give it up, and I told him that I hated to give up my bread. I am very sorry I left my blanket, but I can use Collins's. He will not be able for service in four or five months. General Cheatham is here on a furlough to get married, I am informed. John Bryson is here. Mr. Mar left this morning. Tell the girls that Collins is looking very anxiously for a letter from them every day. The boys here are trying to persuade me not to go in the army. I tell them I have started and I will not back out. Willie McEwin and James Wood are going with me. Willie McEwin is going to the same company to which I am going. The people are expecting a raid here every minute. They have burned the bridge ten miles above Griffin, and are now destroying the railroad. Companies have been sent out to drive the invading party back. There is no more news concerning the army as far as I can ascertain. Capt. Tully is out from Tennessee. He brings no news concerning the family. Collins, I think, will be able to get about in five or six weeks, as the symptoms of the gangrene have ceased. Pa's health is good. When you write, direct your letter to the Eighth Tennessee, care of Col. Anderson, Company E, Atlanta. Write soon. Tell the girls to write to me; but if they don't want to write don't ask them. Collins sends his love. Give my love to the family.

The last wishes of your friend,
John M. Bright, Jr.

P. S. – Tell Uncle Morgan I looked for him in Macon, but couldn't find him. I will proceed to the front to-morrow.

From One of My Wounded Soldiers

In Camp Near Shelbyville, Tenn.,
February 16 1863.

To Mr. Irby Morgan and family.

Kind and Much Esteemed Friends: Ere this you doubtless think I have forgotten you, but far from it. I would have written to you before this time had I had an opportunity of delivering the package you intrusted to my care. Immediately on my arrival I made inquiries and ascertained that Wheeler's command had moved forward, destination unknown. Since then the weather has rendered the roads almost impassable. In a few days I will avail some opportunity to send or take it to the proper one. I met Mr. Herron this morning. He looks well. Mr. Brooks is now in my tent. He is quite well, and sends kindest wishes and regards. The general health of the troops is good. I learn the small-pox is prevalent in some regiments. I hope it will not get around among ours; if it does, I will light out, or be inclined to do so. Light out is the Rebel term of skedaddle. From the present signs of the times, I judge that as soon as the weather admits we will have a fight here. From accounts the enemy moved thirteen divisions from Murfreesboro a short time ago. The weather, though, stops their movements for awhile.

Not being anxious for the conflict, I would not care if it remained so for some time to come. We occasionally hear cannon on the front. It is supposed to be cavalry skirmishing. I heard several this morning. I learn that our regiment and the 13th are to be consolidated. I dislike it very much, though the 13th is a good regiment, or the remainder of one. After the consolidation it will still remain the 154th.

The sharpshooters of our brigade, a company that formerly belonged to our regiment, have been transferred to Forrest's and are to be mounted. They left this morning for Franklin to join Forrest's command. This will be news to Stoveall and Walker. This is about all the news in camp. I never before saw camp so dull, nothing transpiring to break the dull monotony. I have several times wished that I had not left the pleasant little place, Marietta, when I did. My entire trip was gloomy and unpleasant, the trains were very much crowded. I got a seat to Chattanooga by playing a very badly wounded leg on the passengers. From Chattanooga I secured a double seat, and kept it too, by the same game. I suffered a great deal, apparently, from my wounded leg.

I stopped at Tullahoma one day. The next day I took the train for Shelbyville, and found the conductor an old friend and acquaintance. I got a seat n the baggage car, and got to Shelbyville about dark. It was snowing hard. I had to walk about three miles to camp in mud knee deep, and since have not been out of sight of camp, except the day of review of our division before Joseph E. Johnston. Not being on review, I got good sight of him. His appearance is fine, his intellectual capacities are in prominent features, and at once revealed to scrutinizing eyes, and I think is equal to the times and emergencies. He says that our corps is the most imposing he ever reviewed. They are drilled, disciplined, and will fight.

You will please remember me to all my inquiring acquaintances and friends. Tell Mr. Frazier I will write to him if ever anything of interest transpires.

I am going to report for duty in the morning, unless my arm, where I was inoculated, grows worse. The only duty we have is to guard two conscript regiments in our brigade, to keep them from deserting. Poor soldiers.

With great respect I remain yours truly,
John H. Lynn.

Camp Near Chattanooga, Tenn.,
July 16, '63.

Mrs. Morgan: My kind and esteemed friend, it may seem ungrateful that I had not heretofore acknowledged the receipt of your very kind letter of the 22d of May. The only excuse I offer is simply this: We were then lying at Shelbyville, and one could write nothing of interest, and even now cannot do much better than to relate old and stale incidents. As for the particulars of the fate of Vicksburg, you are possibly better acquainted with than I.

The fall of Charleston is reported as truth, yet nothing to confirm the report. Therefore I still have hope that the South can yet boast of one Gibraltar. On or about the 24th of June we were then in front of Shelbyville working on the fortifications. About that time Col. Morgan's "Regiment of Cavalry" moved in near the works about one-half mile from our encampment, but from the push of work I did not get a chance to go and see him, as I would like to have done. On the night of the 26th we got orders to cook rations. About sunrise on the 27th we were formed, not knowing where we were going, to the front or rear. We struck the pike, moved by the left flank, to the rear, in retreat. This day was a hot, sultry one. As we passed through Shelbyville we saw every indication of retreat. Union families were seen peeping through windows exuberant with glee; other families of Southern sympathy were in great distress and gloom. I then thought of yourself and family, feeling as if every foot we moved would prolong your banishment from your once pleasant and happy home. We marched all day in the rear of the army, and night found us seven or eight miles from

Shelbyville, worn-out and sick. During the night the rain fell in torrents, and the only shelter was trees. On the 28th we arrived at Tullahoma, cooked four days' rations on the 29th, and moved to the front on pickets three miles from the line of fortifications – just our brigade – the enemy showing evidence of fight. We occasionally heard a bullet pass. It seemed they were advancing, but slow and cautious. On the 30th the First Kentucky Cavalry had drawn back to our line of skirmishers, and reported the enemy in force two hundred yards from us. We remained thus until after sunset, when a report from a rifle in our front, then a volley which we didn't answer, expecting the enemy wanted to advance his lines. At dark all was quiet as death. We laid down upon our arms with sad feelings, thinking that the dawn of July 1st would usher us on a field of death and carnage. About 10 o'clock we are aroused from sleep and move to the rear, it having been ascertained that Rosey had evaded us by the right flank, and was endeavoring to get to the mountains before we could. We marched all night and until noon of the 2d. We halted at Alizonia, nothing unusual but the heat, and a great many cases of sunstroke. The 3d, at daylight, we moved through Winchester, stopping within two miles of town to rest in the heat of the day. Before we got seated the cavalry were skirmishing in Winchester. We pushed on, got to Cowan Station at 3 or 4 o'clock, formed line of battle, and lay without any further molestation. The 4th day of July we made an early start over the mountains, the enemy's cavalry still pushing us closely until we crossed the mountain and Tennessee River. We were then more secure, all the wagons safe in camp at Shell Mound Springs, which is large enough to float a large boat, and very cold. On the 5th we crossed one mountain, climbed another, and camped on the mountain thirteen miles from this place. On the 6th we got on the railroad, arriving here to learn of the fall of Vicksburg. The troops do not seem so much affected by the intelligence as would be supposed. The consolation is: the gallant conduct of the heroic garrison, and the hardships they underwent before the place surrendered, and the loss the enemy sustained there. It has cost them more than it can be worth, as it does not insure them the free navigation of the Mississippi River. Well, we are lying under the summit of old Lookout, but do not expect to remain, as we have got work to do, and the sooner the better for us. There is no doubt that the enemy will find it easier to recruit since our late reverses.

Mrs. Morgan, I expected Mr. Pettit or Walker to bring me some clothes that my friend, Mrs. Glover, has made for me, but I was disappointed. John Walker certainly forgot it. If you will have them at the hotel at your room, a friend of mine, Mr. Pratt, will bring them to me. He left this morning for Atlanta. Will return Saturday, when he will step off the train to get the package. He would not have time to find Mrs. Glover's house. If you will attend to this request, it will greatly oblige me. Mr. Lowe is driving around camp in good health; Brooks "ditto." I see Lowe occasionally; he is on some detail duty. There is not much sickness at present among the troops, though a great deal of playing off. I have a notion of playing rheumatism for a few days' leave of absence. Bragg says a man is not a good soldier unless he can play off. Tell Fannie I have waited patiently for an answer to a letter written last winter. I am afraid the good people of Marietta are forgetting the situation of their beloved country. I learn they have balls often, and are enjoying the gay frivolities of times of peace. Well, I guess it may be all right, as the first night I was at home in Kentucky I passed at a ball for a few hours, forgetting we were at war, and enjoyed myself beyond description. Give friends, one and all, my kindest regards, and write soon. Remember me to yourself and family.

Your true friend,
J. H. Lynn,
Company E, 154th Tennessee Regiment, T. V.

THE VIDETTE

☆ ☆ ☆ ☆

In these pages we give a portion of the contents of one number of a little paper called *The Vidette*, which was occasionally issued by Gen. Morgan's men while on their rapid march. This copy was printed at Hartsville, Tenn., August 24, 1862; and we reproduce it here, thinking it may be of interest to some of the old soldiers and many of the sons of those gallant men who gave their lives in the defense of the Southern cause.

Morgan's Visit to Gallatin and the Junction – His Fight With Gen. R. W. Johnson

Gen. Morgan, with a portion of his command, marched in the direction of Gallatin, on the 19th inst., and learning that the enemy was moving into the place he ordered Capt. Hutchison with his company to cut them off from Nashville by destroying the bridge, which he did.

Gen. Morgan moved early on the morning of the 20th to engage the Federals, whom he thought gallant enough to meet him. But what was our surprise to learn on reaching Gallatin that the cowards had contented themselves with visiting distress and misery upon the citizens of that town. These hirelings of the North had arrested every male citizen of the town that could be found. The gray haired grandfathers, fathers, husbands, brothers, and sons were torn away from their families because they had fed, or talked with, or seen Morgan and his men. The heartrending appeals of the distressed ones mourning for those who were hurried in the dead hour of night, on foot, to a distant prison, without crime, brought tears to the eyes of many a stout heart besides Morgan's. If Morgan stays his hand when the invader treats our citizens thus, and tries still to abide the rules of civilized warfare, our consolation is that there is a God who looks deep into the heart, who will bless the noble patriot for his forbearance, while he will as surely curse the foul persecutors of quiet men, women, and children. Gen. Morgan could have swept more than one hundred and sixty of them that day from the face of the earth; but no, he captured them. He would not yet turn a deaf ear to their appeals, notwithstanding that they had murdered two of our men in cold blood after they had surrendered, and the cries of those who had appealed in vain were still ringing in his ears. Take care, invaders! I heard a humble minister of the gospel who had witnessed your proceedings say that he hated you now with a bitter hatred.

Gen. Morgan pursued the enemy, who had left about 11 o'clock the night previous on foot, toward Nashville, skirmishing on the right and left, killing about twenty, capturing one hundred and sixty and a few of the stolen negroes, and releasing fifty or more of the citizens of Gallatin. When within nine miles of Nashville, in an advance movement made by Company A upon a stockade where a force of the enemy were posted, Lieut. James A.

Smith, of Company A, and Capt. Gordon E. Niles, former editor of this paper, fell at their posts. Long will they live in the memory of their associates in arms, with whom they nobly battled for Southern rights. Their monument is more imperishable than marble. Gen. Morgan, 'tis said, when a large body surrendered, exclaimed: "Why don't you fight?" No wonder; for that was the feeling of all: disappointment at not getting a chance at men who would attack unarmed citizens and surrender to armed troops. But the basest of all was Col. Heffernan's order to them to kill all the prisoners if attacked by the Confederates.

Gen. Morgan, according to previous arrangement, moved back with his command to Gallatin, after destroying another bridge, more effectually cutting off the communication between Nashville and Louisville. Early on the following morning (the 21st) while preparing to leave Gallatin, our scouts and pickets brought news of the advance of the enemy from toward Hartsville, and soon Gen. Johnson appeared with his forces in sight of town. Gen. Morgan moved his command out of town to meet the enemy. (How unlike the invaders, who take shelter when convenient!) Gen. Morgan gave the gallant Texas boys under Maj. Gano the privilege of opening the fight with the advance of the enemy, which they did in elegant style. Maj. Gano led them forward, while his men poured the contents of their trusty guns into the ranks of the enemy, driving them back under a heavy fire. Upon the left Capts. Castle, Bowles, Castleman, Jennings, and Lieut. White led their companies forward in splendid style under command of Col. Duke, spreading dismay through the right wing of the enemy's ranks; while Capts. Desha, Breckinridge, McFarland, Jones, and Lieut. Lea upon the right, pushing on in gallant style, drove back the enemy's left. Gen. Morgan was seen upon all parts of the field, his voice and presence giving strength to his troops and weakening his foes. Col. St. Leger Grenfell, on the right, cheered on the brave Southrons. Maj. Gano, leading a charge across a field, had his horse killed under him, and the brave Capt. John M. Huffman nobly did his duty upon every charge until a Minie ball fractured his left arm near the shoulder, thus disabling for a time a gallant soldier. After driving the enemy back some three miles from the town, routing them alternately from field and pasture, Gen. Morgan turned back his command to look after the dead and wounded, and after making ample preparation for the interment of the dead and giving attention to the wounded of both friends and foes, and learning that the enemy had formed again some three miles from town, Gen. Morgan advanced to meet them. Throwing Col. Duke with two companies on the right of the pike, Maj. Morgan the left, while Maj. Gano with four companies went forward upon the road, led by the general in person. The enemy fled and divided. Col. Duke followed a heavy force that rallied at Cairo and gave battle. He charged them with his gallant braves, and I have been informed that the firing was as heavy for a short time on the limited field as on the fatal day at Shiloh: but the enemy was routed, and Gen. Johnson captured. The central division pursued another body of the enemy to a ford on the Cumberland River, and firing upon the rear guard killed one horse. The casualties of the day were: In Morgan's command, 8 killed and 12 wounded; in the enemy's ranks, 63 killed (6 since died), about 100 wounded and 200 captured.

The difference between the casualties of the South and North can be easily accounted for: the patriot who fights in defense of his country is nerved to a steady arm under any circumstances. The subjugator, who would conquer in order to play the despot, or fights for hire, trembles for his life. Again, the interposition of divine aid has always been for the DEFENDERS OF JUST RIGHTS, and never with the invader, who battles for subjugation. My firm conviction is that before the South is subjugated there will be none left in the North but women and children. The North could stop the war; the South can continue it as long as the North wishes. Gen. Morgan is here and will remain as long as he chooses, and when he leaves he will take the road to the place of his destination.

An Eyewitness.

Brigade Orders

Headquarters Morgan's Brigade,
Hartsville, Tenn., Aug. 22, 1862.

1. The officer in command calls the attention of all officers and men to the Proclamation issued this day. At the same time he desires to place upon record in Brigade Orders his high sense of the gallantry and devotion shown by all ranks during the two arduous days of service. Soldiers, your commanding officer is proud of you, and thanks you from his heart.

2. The commanding officer having thought it to be to the interest of the service that a corps of guides or scouts should be organized for the more regular and efficient discharge of this most important duty, has ordered that a corps of sixteen men be raised from the several companies under his command, to be commanded

by Lieut. Brady, of Company M, who will select the men most suitable for the service, and present them to the acting brigade general for his approval.

3. Lieut. Brady is hereby withdrawn from Company M, and appointed chief of this newly raised corps, with rank of second lieutenant.

4. Regimental officers are requested for the future to grant no passes or leave of absence except to such soldiers as exhibit their arms in perfect order. The safety of the brigade may often depend upon the state of its arms, and too much attention cannot be paid by regimental officers to this most important duty.

Capt. Jones,
Captain of the Day.

By order of G. St. L. Grenfell.

Editorials

Advices from Nashville show that Johnson's men were picked, and that they have been a month picking and drilling men and horses to take Morgan. Send your refuse next time; your picked men fail.

A report from Nashville last night confirms the statement that Bragg has whipped Buell and captured most of his forces, and that Nelson is trying to find his way out from Nashville with two thousand infantry and two hundred cavalry.

Johnson's men, *en route* for Gallatin, said: "Morgan's men can destroy bridges, but they can't stand fire."

Johnson's men, *en route* for the guardhouse, said:
"Johnson was a fool for attacking Morgan."

———————

The Northern generals have come to the conclusion that their troops are giving their parole to get out of
service. You need not talk any more about volunteers
when you can't keep those you already have in the field
according to your own showing, and if you force back the
paroled soldiers as you threaten to do, you force them to
certain death if captured. So think twice before you act
on that.

———————

Verily the Southern women think every man
good-looking that stands up nobly for his rights. Won't
Morgan have a pretty lot of boys? They improve every
trip. We heard a lady complimenting St. Leger. Some of
the rest of us will come in soon for a share.

———————

We were pleased to see Gen. Forrest yesterday. He
looks to be in the enjoyment of excellent health, and
happy as you could expect so noble a patriot, enjoying the
good news that crowds upon us from every quarter. I
thought as I looked upon the manly forms of Forrest and
Morgan that nothing could excel that picture except the
groups, everywhere to be seen, of our lovely country-
women. They excel all that the universe contains. Untiring
in their efforts, beautifully flushed with the rosy tinge
inspired by patriotic zeal, their warm hearts pouring out
to God unceasing prayers for our success, O what can
equal the women of the South? They are the noblest works

of God. I must leave this dull sanctum to look once more upon them.

––––––––––

Headquarters Morgan's Regiment
Hartsville, August 22, 1862

To Gen. Cooper, Adjutant General, Richmond.

General: I beg to confirm my dispatch of the 20th inst., announcing the result of yesterday's expedition.

My command consisted of my own regiment (seven hundred strong) and a squadron of Texas Rangers, numbering about one hundred men, that returned that day worn-out to Gallatin.

At 11 o'clock P.M. I received information from one of my friendly scouts that the enemy's cavalry was encamped on the roadside between Castalian Springs and Hartsville, a distance of only twelve miles from my camp. Judging from the fact that they had halted by the roadside, I concluded that they intended to march at night or possibly early in the morning, and I made my preparations accordingly, dispatching scouts upon whom I could depend to bring me positive information as to the enemy's movements.

At daybreak my column was on the move, and as the advanced guard reached the head of the town my pickets came galloping in, followed by my principal scout, who reported that he was closely pursued by a large body of cavalry. Not wishing, on account of the inhabitants, to make Gallatin the scene of our contest, I advanced my column, and was greeted on reaching the Hartsville pike by a heavy fire from that direction. I dismounted two leading companies to fight, and threw them into the woods on the left of the road. The enemy increased the fire, and I gradually had my whole command engaged.

The fight began at 6:30 o'clock and was maintained without much advantage on either side – the enemy having, perhaps, rather the best of it at first – until about 8:30 o'clock, when they began to fall back, and my men to redouble their efforts. At 9:30 o'clock I had driven them four miles, and was preparing for a final charge, when a flag of truce was brought proposing an armistice, in order to bury their dead. My reply was, that I could entertain no proposition except unconditional surrender.

I learned then that the troops were commanded by Brig. Gen. Johnson. During the parley, the enemy had formed into line of battle, and were evidently ready to defend themselves from any fresh attack.

I divided my forces into three divisions, leading one myself in the direction which I thought Gen. Johnson had taken. Maj. Morgan had five companies under his orders on my left. Lieut. Col. Duke, on my right, had three companies and his advanced guard.

Some delay was occasioned by the nonarrival of my gallant Texas Rangers, who formed part of the body under my own immediate orders. They had been separated from their horses during the preceding fight, and had not been able to recover them in time to come to the front. On their arrival, we marched on in the direction of the enemy, and Col. Duke's Division coming within sight, advanced at a canter and opened fire. Gen. Johnson's forces, being on a good pike, retreated for some time faster than my men, who were on difficult ground, could follow; but after a pursuit of some two miles they were overtaken and compelled to fight. They were dismounted and formed behind their horses. The position that they had selected was a very good one, especially as they considerably outnumbered Col. Duke's force, which was the only one opposed to them, Maj. Morgan and my own attachment in the eagerness of pursuit having taken too far to the left.

Col. Duke reports that on perceiving that the enemy had halted, he formed his three companies and the advanced guard into columns of squadrons, reserving the regular distances betwixt each so as to be able to form into line at command and attack. This was done with admirable precision and coolness by his men, and nothing could exceed their gallantry.

The enemy was formed under the brow of a hill, and my men were drawn up above them, so that their fire told with effect on my line, whilst that of the attacking party went over their heads. After a very sharp engagement of about fifteen minutes they broke and ran.

Gen. Johnson, his adjutant general, Capt. Turner, Maj. Winfrey, and a number of privates were captured, but the main body escaped to the hills through the woods and high corn, making for the Cumberland River.

Thus ended an action in which my command, not exceeding seven hundred men (one whole company being in the rear with prisoners), succeeded in defeating a brigade of twelve hundred chosen cavalry sent by Gen. Buell expressly to take me or drive me out of Tennessee, killing and wounding some one hundred and eighty, and taking two hundred prisoners, including the brigadier general commanding, and the greater part of the regimental officers.

My loss in both actions amounted to five killed, eighteen wounded, and two missing. Amongst the wounded was Capt. Huffman, who had his arm shattered by a ball whilst leading gallantly on his brave Texas Rangers, a small body of men commanded by Maj. Gano, of whom I cannot speak too highly, as they have distinguished themselves ever since they joined my command, not only by their bravery, but by their good, soldier-like conduct.

To all my officers and men my best acknowledgments are due. Nothing but hard fighting carried them through.

To my personal staff I am deeply indebted. Col. St. Leger acting adjutant general, ably supported me; Capt. Llewellen, my quartermaster, and Capt. Green Roberts, who acted as my aide-de-camp, were most active and fearless in carrying my orders, and the captains of companies were cool and collected in the performance of them.

Lieut. Col. Duke led on his regiment, if possible, with more than his usual gallantry, and contributed by the confidence with which he has inspired his men to insure the success of the day.

Lieut. Col. Duke makes particular mention of the cool and determined manner in which Lieut. Rogers, commanding advanced guard, Capts. Hutchinson, Castle, and Lieut. White, respectively commanding the three companies composing his division, behaved; in fact, the conduct of both officers and men deserves the highest praise.

I received every assistance from the patriotism and zeal of the neighboring citizens, amongst whom Maj. Duffey and Capt. R. A. Bennet were preëminent.

I have also to report that I have received a dispatch from Gen. Forrest stating that he has encamped within eight miles of me with a reënforcement of eight hundred men, but no artillery. The want of this arm cripples my movements and prevents my advance with that certainty of effect which a battery would afford.

Recruits are daily and hourly arriving. The population seems at last to be thoroughly aroused, and to be determined on resistance.

I hope shortly, general, to be able to report further successes; and rest assured that no exertion on my part shall be wanting, and that no sacrifices on that of my officers and men will prevent our giving as good an account of the enemy as our small numbers will admit of.

I have the honor to be, with the greatest respect, general, your most obedient servant,

John H. Morgan,
Colonel Commanding Cavalry, C.S.A.

P. S. – This morning I received positive information as to Gen. Nelson's intentions and movements. He is retreating from Nashville to reënforce Bowling Green, at the head of fifteen hundred infantry, two hundred cavalry, and twelve cannon. It is evident that the intention of the Federals is to attempt the defense of the line at Bowling Green and Lebanon.

J. H. M.

Notices

Quartermaster's Department
Locke's Hotel, Aug. 19, 1862.
All persons having claims against the quartermaster are notified to present them for settlement immediately.

D. H. Llewellyn,
Quartermaster, C.S.A.

Headquarters Morgan's Brigade
Hartsville, August 22, 1862

All persons having property in their possession captured from the enemy will deliver it to me at Locke's hotel.

D.H. Llewellyn,
Assistant Quartermaster, C.S.A.

Proclamation

Headquarters Morgan's Brigade
Hartsville, August 22, 1862.

Soldiers: Your gallant bearing during the last two days will not only be inscribed in the history of the country and the annals of this war, but is engraven deeply in my heart.

Your zeal and devotion on the 20th at the attack of the trestlework at Saundersville, and of the Springfield Junction stockade, your heroism during the two hard fights of yesterday have placed you high on the list of those patriots who are now in arms for our Southern rights.

All communication cut off betwixt Gallatin and Nashville, a body of three hundred infantry totally cut up or taken prisoners, the liberation of those kind friends arrested by our revengeful foes for no other reason than their compassionate care of our sick and wounded, would have been laurels sufficient for your brows. But soldiers, the utter annihilation of Gen. Johnson's brigade, composed of twenty-four picked companies of regulars, and sent on purpose to take us, raises your reputation as soldiers, and strikes fear into the craven hearts of your enemies. Gen. Johnson and his staff, with two hundred men, taken prisoners, sixty-four killed and one hundred wounded, attests the resistance made, and bears testimony to your valor.

But our victories have not been achieved without loss. We have to mourn some brave and dear comrades. Their names will remain in our breasts; their fame outlives them. They died in defense of a good cause. They died, like gallant soldiers, with their front to the foe.

Officers and men, your conduct makes me proud to command you. Fight always as you fought yesterday, and you are invincible.

John H. Morgan,
Colonel Commanding Cavalry.

The End.